KONGI'S HARVEST

Kongi's Harvest is to be the official start of the Five Year Plan. President Kongi has the spiritual leader King Danlola under preventive detention. He is anxious that Danlola should be seen by the people at the festival to bring him the new yam with his own hands. With Danlola and Kongi increasingly involved in image building, the festival comes to a shattering climax.

The play has all the bite of Chaplin's *Great Dictator*, especially in the scenes in which Kongi is building his image; Kongi's 'last supper' poses for an international photographer; the argument about which member of the Reformed Aweri community should write his book; pictures of Kongi's Terminus, Kongi's University and Kongi's Refineries; and the decision to date the years from Kongi's Harvest.

'Wole Soyinka has done for our napping language what brigand dramatists from Ireland have done for centuries; booted it awake, rifled its pockets and scattered the loot into the middle of next week. . . .' Thus *The Observer*, London, in 1965 greeted the Commonwealth Arts Festival production of Wole Soyinka's previous play *The Road*; at the First Festival of the Negro Arts at Dakar it was awarded the prize for published drama. *Kongi's Harvest* has possibly even greater dramatic potential.

Wole Soyinka, born in 1934, studied at the Universities of Ibadan and Leeds. He spent 18 months at the Royal Court Theatre, London, as a play reader before returning to Nigeria in 1960 to start 'The 1960 Masks' and, later, 'The Orisun Theatre'. He has held research and teaching appointments at the Universities of Ife, Ibadan, and Lagos.

D0218690

Wole Soyinka

KONGI'S HARVEST

———————✳——————

Oxford University Press

Oxford University Press, Walton Street, Oxford OX2 6DP

OXFORD   NEW YORK   TORONTO
DELHI   BOMBAY   CALCUTTA   MADRAS   KARACHI
PETALING JAYA   SINGAPORE   HONG KONG   TOKYO
NAIROBI   DAR ES SALAAM   CAPE TOWN
MELBOURNE   AUCKLAND

and associated companies in
BERLIN   IBADAN

Oxford is a trade mark of Oxford University Press

ISBN 0 19 911085 9

First published 1967
Fourteenth impression 1992

This play is fully protected by copyright and all
applications for public performance should be made to
Oxford University Press
Walton Street, Oxford OX2 6DP

Cover illustration
by Jimo Akolo

Printed in Hong Kong

Characters

OBA DANLOLA	*a traditional ruler*
SARUMI	*a junior Oba*
DAODU	*son to Sarumi and heir to Danlola's throne*
OGBO AWERI	*Head of the Oba's defunct Conclave of Elders*
DENDE	*servant to Danlola*
SEGI	*a courtesan, Kongi's ex-mistress*
KONGI	*President of Isma*
ORGANISING SECRETARY	
FIRST AWERI	
SECOND AWERI	
THIRD AWERI	*members of the Reformed Aweri*
FOURTH AWERI	*Fraternity*
FIFTH AWERI	
SIXTH AWERI	

SUPERINTENDENT CAPTAIN OF THE CARPENTER'S BRIGADE
RIGHT AND LEFT EARS OF STATE

Retinue, Drummers, Praise-singers, the Carpenters' Brigade, Photographer, night-club habituées.

The action takes place on the eve and the day of the national celebrations of Isma.

Kongi's Harvest was first performed in August 1965 in Lagos by the 1960 MASKS AND ORISUN Theatre.

HEMLOCK

*A roll of drums such as accompanies a national anthem. Presumably
the audience will rise. The curtain rises with them. Grouped
solemnly behind it are Oba Danlola, Wuraola his favourite wife,
his Ogbo Aweri, Dende and Danlola's retinue of drummers and
buglers. They break into the following anthem:*

> The pot that will eat fat
> Its bottom must be scorched
> The squirrel that will long crack nuts
> Its footpad must be sore
> The sweetest wine has flowed down
> The tapper's shattered shins
> And there is more, oh-oh
> Who says there isn't more
> Who says there isn't plenty a word
> In a penny newspaper
>
> Ism to ism for ism is ism
> Of isms and isms on absolute-ism
> To demonstrate the tree of life
> Is sprung from broken peat
> And we the rotted bark, spurned
> When the tree swells its pot
> The mucus that is snorted out
> When Kongi's new race blows
> And more, oh there's a harvest of words
> In a penny newspaper
>
> They say, oh how
> They say it all on silent skulls

But who cares? Who but a lunatic
Will bandy words with boxes
With government rediffusion sets
Which talk and talk and never
Take a lone word in reply.

I cannot counter words, oh
I cannot counter words of
A rediffusion set
My ears are sore
But my mouth is *agbayun*
For I do not bandy words
No I do not bandy words
With a government loudspeaker.

SUPERINTENDENT [*rushes in, agitated.*]: Kabiyesi, be your age.
These antics may look well on a common agitator but
really, an elder is an elder, and a king does not become a
menial just because he puts down his crown to eat.

DANLOLA [*to the beat of* gbedu *drum, steps into slow, royal dance.*]:
E ma gun' yan Oba kere o
E ma gun' yan Oba kere
Kaun elepini ko se e gbe mi
Eweyo noin ni i fi i yonu
E ma gun' yan Oba kere

Don't pound the king's yam
In a small mortar
Don't pound the king's yam
In a small mortar
Small as the spice is
It cannot be swallowed whole
A shilling's vegetable must appease
A halfpenny spice.

SUPERINTENDENT: It won't work, Kabiyesi, it won't work.

Every evening you gather your friends together and
desecrate the National Anthem. It has to stop!

SARUMI: *Oba ni i f'epo inu ebo ra'ri*
Orisa l'oba
Oba ni i f'epo inu ebo r'awuje
Orisa l'oba.

None but the king
Takes the oil from the crossroads
And rubs it in his *awuje*
The king is a god.

SUPERINTENDENT: I say you desecrate our National Anthem. I
have to do something about it. And stop that unholy noise.
[*Seizes the lead drummer by the wrist. Everything stops.
Complete silence.*]

DANLOLA [*slowly.*]: You stopped the royal drums?

SUPERINTENDENT: I shall speak to the Secretary about this . . .

DANLOLA [*suddenly relaxed.*]: No, it is nothing new. Your betters
Stopped the drums a long time ago
And you the slave in khaki and brass buttons
Now lick your masters' spit and boast,
We chew the same tobacco.

SUPERINTENDENT. [*turning to Sarumi.*]: Look, you better warn
him . . .

SARUMI. We do not hear the jackal's call
When the Father speaks.

SUPERINTENDENT: This cannot continue. I shall insist that the
Secretary put you all in different sections of the camp. This
cannot go on.

DANLOLA: Good friend, you merely stopped
My drums. But they were silenced
On the day when Kongi cast aside
My props of wisdom, the day he
Drove the old Aweri from their seats.

What is a king without a clan
Of Elders? What will Kongi be without . . .
Sarumi, what name was it again?

SARUMI: The Reformed Aweri Fraternity.

DANLOLA: A big name for little heads.
And now, he wants to eat
The first of the New Yam. The mashed
Weak yams on which the crow
Weaned our Leader his son still stick
Between his teeth and prove too tough
For his adult comfort, but he seeks
To eat the first of the New Yam.

[*The retainers burst into derisive laughter and the Superintendent becomes incensed.*]

SUPERINTENDENT: You see if I don't do something about that subversive kind of talk. . . . E-eh!

[*He looks down and sees for the first time what Danlola has used for a wrapper under his agbada. Looks rapidly up at a flagpole in the middle of the yard and back again to Danlola's legs.*]

SUPERINTENDENT: Kabiyesi, is that not our national flag?

DANLOLA: Did you not deprive me of my national trousers?

SUPERINTENDENT: Yes, to keep you from escaping.

DANLOLA: The nude shanks of a king
Is not a sight for children—
It will blind them.
When an Oba stops the procession
And squats on the wayside,
It's on an urgent matter
Which spares neither king nor god.
Wise heads turn away
Until he's wiped his bottom.

SUPERINTENDENT [*wildly.*]: We'll soon see about that. You want to cost me my job do you?

[*He rushes at Danlola and whips off the flag. Danlola first rapidly gathers his agbada round his legs to protect his semi-nudity, then shrugs and tries to assume a dignified indifference.*]

DANLÓLA: It was our fathers who said, not I—
A crown is a burden when
The king visits his favourite's
Chambers. When the king's wrapper
Falls off in audience, wise men know
He wants to be left alone. So—
[*Shoos him off with a contemptuous gesture.*]

SUPERINTENDENT [*going.*]: Too much indulgence, that's why.
It's all the fault of the Organising Secretary permitting
your wives and all these other creatures to visit you. And
you are not even grateful.

DANLOLA [*bursts into laughter.*] We curse a wretch denying cause
For gratitude deserved, but it is
A mindless clown who dispenses
Thanks as a fowl scatters meal
Not caring where it falls. Thanks?
In return for my long fingers of largesse
Your man knows I love to have my hairs
Ruffled well below the navel.
Denied that, are you or he the man
To stop me breaking out of camp?
And granting my retainers leave
To keep me week-end company—is that also
Reason for the grass to tickle [*slapping his belly.*]
The royal wine-gourd? Well?
What says the camp superintendent?
Shall I...?
[*Makes a motion as if he means to prostrate himself.*]

RETAINERS [*step forward, shouting in alarm.*]: Ewo!★

DANLOLA: But he says I must. Let me
Prostrate myself to him.

★Taboo.

[*Again the gesture. He and his retainers get involved in a mock-struggle.*]

SUPERINTENDENT: I did not make any impious demand of you.
　　All I asked was for more respect to constituted authority.
　　I didn't ask for a curse on my head.

DANLOLA: Curse? Who spoke of curses?
　　To prostrate to a loyal servant
　　Of Kongi—is that a curse?

SUPERINTENDENT: Only a foolish child lets a father prostrate to
　　him. I don't ask to become a leper or a lunatic. I have no
　　wish to live on sour berries.

DANLOLA: All is well. The guard has waived
　　His rights and privileges. The father
　　Now prostrates himself in gratitude.

SUPETINTENDENT [*shouting.*]: I waived nothing. I had nothing to
　　waive, nothing to excuse. I deny any rights and beg you
　　not to cast subtle damnations on my head.

DANLOLA: Oh but what a most suspicious mould
　　Olukori must have used for casting man.
　　Subtle damnations? If I was
　　Truly capable of that, would I
　　Now be here, thanking you for little
　　Acts of kindness flat on my face?
　　[*Again his act.*]

SUPERINTENDENT [*forestalls him by throwing himself down.*]:
　　I call you all to witness. Kabiyesi, I am only the fowl
　　droppings that stuck to your slippers when you strolled
　　in the back yard. The child is nothing; it is only the
　　glory of his forebears that the world sees and tolerates
　　in him.

SARUMI: Ah, don't be angry with him
　　Oba Danlola, don't be angry
　　With your son. If the baobab shakes
　　Her head in anger, what chance

Has the rodent when
An ear-ring falls
And hits the earth with thunder.

DANLOLA [*swelling, swelling....*]:
He paraded me to the world
L'ogolonto★ I leave this abuse
To the judgement of the....

SUPERINTENDENT: Please—plead with him. Intercede for me.

SARUMI: Kabiyesi, a father employs only a small stick on his
child, he doesn't call in the policemen to take him to gaol.
Don't give voice to the awesome names on an Oba's
tongue; when you feel kinder, they cannot easily be re-
called. They must fulfil what task they were called to do.
[*The retainers intervene, pleading with Danlola. His drummers
try to soothe him and Wura kneels to placate his anger.
Gradually he calms down, slowly, as Sarumi sings.*]

SARUMI: Ah, Danlola, my father,
Even so did I
Wish your frown of thunder away
When the Aweri were driven from
Their ancient conclave. Then you said, ...

DRUMMER: This is the last
That we shall dance together
They say we took too much silk
For the royal canopy
But the dead will witness
We never ate the silkworm.

SARUMI: They complained because
The first of the new yams
Melted first in an Oba's mouth
But the dead will witness
We drew the poison from the root.
[*As the King's men begin a dirge of ege, Danlola sits down*

★Stark naked.

slowly onto a chair, withdrawing more and more into himself.]

DRUMMER: I saw a strange sight
   In the market this day
   The day of the feast of Agemo
   The sun was high
   And the King's umbrella
   Beneath it. . . .

SARUMI: We lift the King's umbrella
   Higher than men
   But it never pushes
   The sun in the face.

DRUMMER: I saw a strange sight
   In the market this day
   The sun was high
   But I saw no shade
   From the King's umbrella.

OGBO AWERI: This is the last
   That we shall dance together
   This is the last the hairs
   Will lift on our skin
   And draw together
   When the *gbedu** rouses
   The dead in *oshugbo*†. . . .

SARUMI: This is the last our feet
   Shall speak to feet of the dead
   And the unborn cling
   To the hem of our robes
   Oh yes, we know they say
   We wore out looms
   With weaving robes for kings
   But I ask, is *popoki*‡,
   The stuff to let down

---

*big ceremonial drum.   †shrine of Oro (cult of the dead).
‡thick coarse, woven cloth.

To unformed fingers clutching up
At life?

OGBO AWERI: Did you not see us
Lead twins by the hand?
Did you not see us
Shade the albino's eyes
From the hard sun, with a fan
Of parrot feathers?
Even so did the god* enjoin
Whose hands of chalk
Have formed the cripple
And the human bat of day.

SARUMI: Don't pound the king's yam
With a small pestle
Let the dandy's wardrobe
Be as lavish as the shop
Of the dealer in brocades
It cannot match an elder's rags.

DANLOLA [almost to himself.]: This dance is the last
Our feet shall dance together
The royal python may be good
At hissing, but it seems
The scorpion's tail is fire.

DRUMMER: The king's umbrella
Gives no more shade
But we summon no dirge-master.
The tunnel passes through
The hill's belly
But we cry no defilement
A new-dug path may lead
To the secret heart of being.
Ogun is still a god
Even without his navel.

*Obatala, a Yoruba deity.

OGBO AWERI: Observe, when the monster child
  Was born, *Opele** taught us to
  Abandon him beneath the buttress tree
  But the mother said, oh no,
  A child is still a child
  The mother in us said, a child
  Is still the handiwork of Olukori.

SARUMI: Soon the head swelled
  Too big for pillow
  And it swelled too big
  For the mother's back
  And soon the mother's head
  Was nowhere to be seen
  And the child's slight belly
  Was strangely distended.

DANLOLA [*comes forward, dancing softly.*]:
  This is the last
  Our feet shall touch together
  We thought the tune
  Obeyed us to the soul
  But the drums are newly shaped
  And stiff arms strain
  On stubborn crooks, so
  Delve with the left foot
  For ill-luck; with the left
  Again for ill-luck; once more
  With the left alone, for disaster
  Is the only certainty we know.

[*The bugles join in royal cadences, the two kings dance slow, mournful steps, accompanied by their retinue. Coming down on the scene, a cage of prison bars separating Danlola from Sarumi and the other visitors who go out backwards herded off by the Superintendent.*]

*vehicle for *Ifa* (divination).

First Part

The action alternates between two scenes, both of which are present on different parts of the stage and are brought into play in turn, by lights. First, Kongi's retreat in the mountains, the Reformed Aweri Fraternity in session. Kongi is seen dimly in his own cell, above the Aweri. Rising slowly, a chant in honour of Kongi.

FOURTH AWERI: We need an image. Tomorrow being our first appearance in public, it is essential that we find an image.

FIFTH: Why?

THIRD: Why? Is that question necessary?

FIFTH: It is. Why do we need an image?

THIRD: Well, if you don't know that. . . .

FOURTH: He doesn't, so I'll answer the question. Especially as he seems to be staying awake at last.

FIFTH: Don't sneer. I've heard your snores twice at least this session.

FOURTH: Kindly return to the theme of this planning session. The problem of an image for ourselves.

SECOND: Isn't it enough just to go in as Kongi's disciples?

FOURTH: Magi is more dignified. We hold after all the position of the wise ones. From the recognition of us as the Magi, it is one step to his inevitable apotheosis.

FIRST: Which is to create a new oppositional force.

SECOND: Kongi is a great strategist. He will not take on too many opponents at once.

FIFTH: I still have not been told why we need an image.

THIRD: You are being very obstructive.

FIFTH: Why do we need an image?

FIRST: I suggest we pattern ourselves on our predecessors. Oh I

do admit they were a little old-fashioned, but they had
er . . . a certain style. Yes, I think style is the word I want.
Style. Yes, I think we could do worse than model
ourselves on the old Aweri.

FIFTH: You mean, speak in proverbs and ponderous tone rhythms?

FOURTH: I'm afraid that is out anyway. Kongi would prefer a
clean break from the traditional conclave of the so-called
wise ones.

FIRST: They were remote, impersonal—we need these aspects.
They breed fear in the common man.

SECOND: The paraphenalia helped too, don't forget that.

SIXTH: I have no intention of making myself look ridiculous in
that outfit.

FOURTH: Welcome back to the discussion. I take it you know the
subject.

SIXTH: No. Enlighten me.

FOURTH: The subject is an image for the Reformed Aweri
Fraternity of which you are a member in your waking
moments.

FIFTH: And why do we need an image?

THIRD: Will you for Kongi's sake stop repeating that question?

FIFTH: When will you learn not to speak for Kongi?

FOURTH: Is this yet another effort to divert this discussion?

FIFTH: There is no discussion. Until Kongi makes up his mind
just what image his is going to be this time, you can do
nothing. I am going back to sleep.

FIRST: The emphasis of our generation is—youth. Our image
therefore should be a kind of youthful elders of the state.
A conclave of modern patriarchs.

THIRD: Yes, yes. Nice word patriarch, I'm glad you used it. Has a
nice, reverent tone about it. Very nice indeed, very nice.

SECOND: I agree. Conjures up quite an idyllic scene.

THIRD: Yes, yes, children handing the patriarch his pipe at
evening, crouching at his feet to sip raindrops of wisdom.

FIFTH: And dodging hot ashes as age shakes his rheumatic hand
and the pipe overturns?

THIRD: You seem to turn a sour tongue on every progress we
make in this discussion. Why don't you simply stay asleep?

FIFTH: When the patriarch overturns his pipe, make way. It is no
time for piety.

THIRD: Well, now you've let off your crosswinds of advice, I
hope your stomach pipes you sweeter to sleep.

FOURTH: We might consider a scientific image. This would be a
positive stamp and one very much in tune with our
contemporary situation. Our pronouncements should be
dominated by a positive scientificism.

THIRD: A brilliant conception. I move we adopt it at once.

SIXTH: What image exactly is positive scientificism?

THIRD: Whatever it is, it is not long-winded proverbs and senile
pronouncements. In fact we could say a step has already
been taken in that direction. If you've read our Leader's
last publication. . . .

FIFTH: Ah yes. Nor proverbs nor verse, only ideograms in
algebraic quantums. If the square of XQY(2bc) equals QA
into the square root of X, then the progressive forces
must prevail over the reactionary in the span of .32 of a
single generation.

FOURTH: I trust you understood that as well as you remember it.

FIFTH: No. As well as *you* understand it.

FOURTH: I've had enough of your negative attitude . . . !

*Coloured lights, and the sustained chord of a juju band guitar gone
typically mad brings on the night club scene, a few dancers on, the band
itself off-stage. Daodu is dancing with Segi.*
*Enter Secretary flanked by the Right and Left Ear of State. Reactions
are immediate to their entry. A few night-lifers pick up their drinks
and go in, there are one or two aggressive departures, some stay on*

defiantly, others obsequiously try to attract attention and say a humble greeting. Daodu and Segi dance on. The music continues in the background.

SECRETARY [*approaches the pair.*]: Like a word with you. In private.

SEGI [*very sweetly.*]: You can see I'm occupied Mr. Secretary.

SECRETARY: I don't mean you. Your boy friend.

SEGI: He's busy too.

SECRETARY: Madam, I haven't come to make trouble.

SEGI [*very gently.*]: You couldn't, even if you wanted. Not here.

SECRETARY: I wouldn't be too sure of that.

SEGI: I would.

DAODU: What do you want with me?

SECRETARY: Not here. Let's find somewhere quiet.

[*Daodu leaves Segi at a table and follows the Secretary.*]

SECRETARY [*with abrupt violence.*]: Your uncle is a pain in the neck.

DAODU: Who?

SECRETARY: Your uncle. You are Daodu aren't you? Son of Sarumi by his wife number six. And Oba Danlola is your uncle and you the heir-apparent to his throne. And I have come to tell you that your uncle is a damned stubborn goat, an obstructive, cantankerous creature and a bloody pain in my neck.

DAODU: I'm sorry to hear that.

SECRETARY: Don't waste my time with apologies. You know who I am of course.

DAODU: I don't believe so.

SECRETARY: Organising Secretary to the Leader. Those two, the Right and the Left Ears of State. The combination keeps the country non-aligned. Understand?

DAODU: I think so.

SECRETARY: And your guardian and uncle, Danlola, is a pain in my neck. Now tell me, what has he up his sleeves?

DAODU: Up his sleeves?

SECRETARY: Up those voluminous sleeves of his. What is he hiding there in for tomorrow?

DAODU: I thought he's been in detention for nearly a year.

SECRETARY: That doesn't stop him from messing me about. It only gives him an alibi.

DAODU: Hadn't you better turn him loose then?

SECRETARY: I might do that. Yes, I might do that. Hm. [*Looks slowly round.*] Does that woman have to keep looking at me like that?

DAODU: Does she bother you?

SECRETARY: Isn't there anywhere else we can go? I need to concentrate.

DAODU: I can ask her to go in if you like.

SECRETARY: Nonsense. Leave her where she is. I just wish she'd ... what do they sing about her? What are they saying?

DAODU: The being of Segi
        Swirls the night
        In potions round my head

        But my complaints
        Will pass.

        It is only
        A madman ranting
        When the lady
        Turns her eyes,

        Fathomless on those
        I summoned as my go-between.

SECRETARY: Elegant. Very elegant. You know, I am very fond of music. Unfortunately I haven't much time for it. Moreover one would hardly wish to be found in this sort of place.

DAODU: But you are here now.

SECRETARY: Yes, but only in the line of duty.

DAODU: You should take your duty more seriously and come more often.

SECRETARY: What? Oh . . . ha . . . ha good idea, good idea.

DAODU: However, what brings you here to see me?

SECRETARY: Ah yes, we must get away from distractions and stick to business. [*Leans forward suddenly.*] But tell me, is she really as dangerous as they say? Some men I know have burns to show for their venture in that direction. The types too you'd think would know their way around.

DAODU: No. Listen to what they're singing now. *They* know Segi.

> The wine-hour wind
> That cools us
> Leaves no prints behind
>
> The spring
> Has travelled long
> To soothe our blistered feet
>
> But last year's sands
> Are still at the source
> Unruffled.

SECRETARY: Just the same I wish she'd stop boring into my neck with her eyes.

DAODU: But she's gone.

SECRETARY [*spins round.*]: When? I didn't see her go.

DAODU: Her presence seemed to disturb you so I asked her to excuse us.

SECRETARY: You did? When?

DAODU: Just now.

SECRETARY [*narrowly.*]: I didn't see or hear you do anything. Are you trying to make a fool of me?

DAODU: No.

SECRETARY: Because I warn you, I'm a very dangerous man. I
  don't care what her reputation is, mine is also something
  to reckon with.

DAODU: Fame, is a flippant lover
  But Segi you made him a slave
  And no poet now can rival
  His devotedness.

  The politician
  Fights for place
  With fat juices
  On the tongue of generations

  The judge
  Is flushed down with wine
  And pissed
  Into the gutter

  But Segi
  You are the stubborn strand
  Of meat, lodged
  Between my teeth

  I picked and picked
  I found it was a silken thread
  Wound deep down my throat
  And makes me sing.

SECRETARY: And make me thirsty, where is the waiter!

DAODU: Just behind you.

SECRETARY: Where? Oh, get us some beer.

DAODU: It's here.

SECRETARY: I don't remember ordering any.

DAODU: Segi did. She looks after her guests, especially important
  ones.

[*Secretary changes his mind about replying, digs instead into his pockets.*]
Naturally, it's on the house.

SECRETARY: No thank you. I prefer to pay for my drinks.

DAODU: The waiter won't take it.

SECRETARY: I hope at least I can buy drinks for my assistants. Where are they anyway?

DAODU: Inside on duty.

SECRETARY: What is that supposed to mean?

DAODU: Keeping their ears open—isn't that what they're paid for? By the way, tell them not to stick their ears out too long or they might get slashed off. People are rather touchy here.

SECRETARY: No need to teach them their job.

DAODU: I thought just I'd mention it. Well, here's to duty.
[*Secretary grunts, drinks with the same pointlessly angry gestures. Lights fade. Kongi's chant. Change of lights into next scene.*]

Secretary speaks as he enters.

SECRETARY: How goes the planning session?

FIFTH: I am starving.

SECRETARY: That is a normal sensation with people who indulge in fasting.

FIFTH: I do not indulge in fasting. I am fasting under duress.

SECRETARY: I know nothing of that.

FIFTH. Nor do I. But you ask my stomach about it.

THIRD: Damn your greedy stomach.
[*Enter Kongi. They rise quickly.*]

KONGI: Do they have all the facts?

SECRETARY: I was just beginning . . .

KONGI: Do it now. There is little time left.

SECRETARY: The Leader's image for the next Five-Year Development Plan will be that of a benevolent father of the nation.

This will be strongly projected at tomorrow's Harvest
festival which has been chosen as the official start to the
Five-Year Plan. They key-word is Harmony. Total
Harmony.

KONGI. I want an immediate disputation on the subject. Then a
planning session. [*Goes off.*]

FIFTH: And what, may I ask, does that mean in practical terms?
What is the obstructive lump?

SECRETARY: Oba Danlola.

SECOND: What! That man again?

SECRETARY: He still refuses to give up the New Yam?

FIRST: Why is it necessary for him to give it up? He's in
detention isn't he?

FIFTH: I could do with a bit of yam right now.

SIXTH: Me too. New or old I couldn't care less.

THIRD: Can't you two shut up your greedy mouths for a
change?

FOURTH: If you can, just for a few moments, I would like to set
the subject up in neat patterns for a formal disputation.
The central problem, I take it, is this reactionary relic of
the Kingship institution.

SECRETARY: If by that you mean Danlola, yes.

FIRST: The man is in P.D. The state has taken over his functions.
What exactly is the problem?

FOURTH: An act of public submission, obviously. Kongi must
have his submission in full view of the people. The
wayward child admits his errors and begs his father's
forgiveness.

FIRST: You'll never do it. I know that stubborn old man, you'll
never do it.

FOURTH: Kongi achieves all.

FIRST: Don't read me that catechism of the Carpenters' Brigade
man. Be practical.

FOURTH: I am being practical. Now let us see the problem as

part of a normal historic pattern. This means in effect that
—Kongi must prevail.

FIFTH: Page Two, section 3b of the Carpenters' Credo.

FOURTH: Look here....

FIFTH: If you must catechise, at least sing it like the Carpenters.
I take it they are the ones waiting from below.

SECOND: It's a horrible noise. I'd like to push a rock down on
their heads.

SIXTH: Couldn't you find another choir to serenade the Leader?

SECRETARY: Gentlemen, please. All we want is some way of
persuading King Danlola to bring the New Yam to Kongi
with his own hands. I have organised the rest—the
agricultural show to select the prize-winning yam, the
feast, the bazaar, the music, the dance. Only one thing is
missing—Oba Danlola. And gentlemen, that problem is
yours. Kongi desires that the King perform all his
customary spiritual functions, only this time, that he
perform them to him, our Leader. Kongi must preside as
the Spirit of Harvest, in pursuance of the Five-Year
Development Plan.

FOURTH: An inevitable stage in the process of power
reversionism.

SECRETARY: Call it what you like. Kongi wants a solution, and
fast.

FOURTH: All right. We will hold a formal disputation.

SECRETARY: And the key-word, Kongi insists, must be—
Harmony. We need that to counter the effect of the recent
bomb-throwing. Which is one of the reasons why the
culprits of that outrage will be hanged tomorrow.

[*A nervous silence. They look at one another, stare at their feet.*]

FOURTH: An exercise in scientific exorcism—I approve.

[*Followed by murmurs and head-nodding of agreement by the
majority.*

Loud chord on guitar and into the next scene.]

Segi's Club

SECRETARY: And what about you sir? What do *you* have in
mind?

DAODU: Me?

SECRETARY: Yes you. Tomorrow is State Festival.

DAODU: The Harvest?

SECRETARY: Naturally.

DAODU: I am looking forward to it. We are bound to take the
first prize for the New Yam.

SECRETARY: Who are we?

DAODU: We? My farm of course. You know I own a farm.

SECRETARY: Of course I know you own a farm. There is very
little I don't know let me tell you. What I don't understand
is . . . no, wait a minute, I like to be sure of my facts before
I jump. Now, did you say you are going to take the first
prize tomorrow?

DAODU: Yes.

SECRETARY: You will compete in the agricultural show?

DAODU: Obviously.

SECRETARY: There is something not quite right somewhere. Or
could it be that you are not yet aware that this time it is not
your uncle who will eat the New Yam, but our Leader.

DAODU: I know all about that. What is it they say . . . the old
order changeth—right?

SECRETARY: Cheers. Wish we had more democratic princes like
you. [*he cheers up considerably.*]
When you think of it, I shouldn't be surprised at all.
There's a lot about you which marks you out to be quite
exceptional. Mind you, I won't deny that once or twice
you actually had us worried. Ye-e-es we really thought
at one stage we would have to do something about you.

DAODU: Why?

SECRETARY: Well . . . [*looks round him.*] I'll be quite honest with

you. We felt you were not quite . . . how should I put it
. . . quite with us, that you were not pulling along with us.
I mean we already had farm co-operatives but you had to
start a farmers' community of your own!

DAODU: But it worked.

SECRETARY: Of course it worked! Damn it man, were you
trying to show us up? [*A waiter refills his glass; he downs it.*]
It was bad for our morale man, really bad.

DAODU: I am sorry to hear that.

SECRETARY [*waves him aside.*]: No you're not. I don't know how
you did it but you got results. And your workers—
contented sows the whole bloody lot of them. Oh our
people sing too, but not in tune if you get my meaning.
See what I mean? Very bad for the morale. Listen, I don't
mind telling you . . . we sent in a few spies just to see what
you were up to, but you know what happened?

DAODU [*mock ignorance.*] No. Tell me.

SECRETARY: They never came back.

DAODU: Really! I am sorry about that.

SECRETARY: Will you stop saying you're sorry! [*Downs the rest
of his beer and calls for more.*] Anyway, we couldn't do much
about you. As long as you were contributing to the
national economy . . . you see, my personal motto is
Every Ismite must do his Mite . . . hey, did you hear that?

DAODU [*looking round*]: What?

SECRETARY: No, me. Didn't you hear what I said. Came out
just now, just like that, spontaneous. Every Ismite must do
his Mite. How is that for a rallying slogan for tomorrow
eh? Find me a pen quickly before it goes. My memory is
like a basket when I've had a few beers.

DAODU: Let me write it for you.
[*Scribbles it on a beer-pad and gives it to him.*]

SECRETARY: Let me read it. Every-Ismite-Must-Do-His-Mite!
Hey, you've added something to it.

DAODU: Don't you like it? I've just thought of it too.

SECRETARY: Ismite-Is-Might! Did you think that up?

DAODU: A moment ago.

SECRETARY: What! You are . . . a prince of slogans. A prince of
slogans. Waiter! Waiter! bring more beer. You know,
this is the most profitable night I've had in a long time.
You wait until I get this to the Leader. [*He rises, flushed
and excited.*] End of the celebrations. Kongi raises his right
fist—his favourite gesture have you noticed? raises his
right fist and says just the one word—Ismite. . . .

LAYABOUTS: Is Might!

SECRETARY: Ismite. . . .

LAYABOUTS: Is Might.

[*More people come in from the club and gather round.*]

SECRETARY: Ismite. . . .

CROWD [*thunderously.*]: Is Might!

[*Stops suddenly, then turns to examine his supporters and sinks
back into his chair, his face wrinkled in disgust.*]

SECRETARY: Does no one come here except prostitutes and cut-
throats?

[*In twos, and threes the habituées melt slowly away.*]

Kongi's Retreat

FOURTH: Now, a systematic examination of the data. What have
we got on our plates?

FIFTH: A few crumbs of mouldy bread isn't it?

THIRD: What did you say?

FIFTH: I said a few crumbs of bread. What else do we ever get
on our plates?

FOURTH: Can't you keep your mind on the subject? I used a
common figure of speech and you leap straight onto the
subject of food.

FIFTH: If your mind wasn't licking round the subject all the time how come you always pick that kind of expression?

SIXTH: He's right. It was a most unfortunate choice of words— what have we got on our plates? After several days of slow starvation what other answer do you expect?

THIRD: Can we return to the subject? We need a way to persuade that old reactionary to. . . .

FIFTH: Starve him. Try starving him to death!

FOURTH: That would hardly solve the problem. It needs a live person to make even a symbolic act of capitulation.

THIRD: Especially when harmony is the ultimate goal. The ultimate goal.

FOURTH: I think I see something of the Leader's vision of this harmony. To replace the old superstitious festival by a state ceremony governed by the principle of Enlightened Ritualism. It is therefore essential that Oba Danlola, his bitterest opponent, appear in full antiquated splendour surrounded by his Aweri Conclave of Elders who, beyond the outward trappings of pomp and ceremony and a regular supply of snuff, have no other interest in the running of the state.

SIXTH: Who says?

FOURTH: Kongi says. The period of isolated saws and wisdoms is over, superseded by a more systematic formulation of comprehensive philosophies—*our* function, for the benefit of those who still do not know it.

THIRD: Hear hear.

FOURTH: And Danlola, the retrogressive autocrat, will with his own hands present the Leader with the New Yam, thereby acknowledging the supremacy of the State over his former areas of authority spiritual or secular. From then on, the State will adopt towards him and to all similar institutions the policy of glamourised fossilism.

THIRD: Hear hear, very precisely put.

SECOND: You still haven't said how you are going to do it?

FOURTH: I beg your pardon.

SECOND: How will you make the king take part in this—public act of submission?

FOURTH: Just what is the difficulty? I have outlined the main considerations haven't I?

SECOND: Outlining the considerations is not exactly a solution.

FOURTH: You all expect me to do all the thinking don't you?

FIFTH: Don't look at me. I've told you I can't think on an empty stomach.

THIRD: Can't you lay off your filthy stomach?

FIFTH: I can't. Why the hell couldn't Kongi do his fasting alone? I'll tell you why. He loves companions in misery.

FIRST: Look man, enough of you. You didn't have to come.

FIFTH: Yah? I'd like to see any of us refusing that order. And anyway, he said nothing of fasting at the time. Just disputations and planning.

SIXTH: Very true. I knew nothing of the fasting part of it until we were cut off from all contact.

THIRD: Don't you arrogate yourselves to being his companions in misery. You get something to eat. Kongi doesn't eat at all.

FIFTH: All part of his diabolical cleverness. A little bit of dry bread every day just to activate the stomach devils. Much better if we'd gone all out like him.

FIRST: Hey, go easy man. You're asking for P.D. if you go on in that tone.

FIFTH: At least you get fed. And if you have money you can live like a king—ask our dear Organising Secretary if you don't believe me.

SECRETARY: You are suggesting something nasty Sir?

FIFTH: Don't act innocent with me. If a detainee pays your price you'll see to his comforts. I bet our royal prisoner has put on weight since he came under your charge.

SECRETARY: This is slander.

FIFTH: Sue me.

SECRETARY: I refuse to listen to any more of this.

FIFTH: And a full sex-life too I bet. Are you going to tell me you don't issue week-end permits to his wives?

SECRETARY: You are taking advantage of your privileged position.

FIFTH: I waive it you shameless bribe-collector. Say whatever is on your mind, or take me to court. I waive my philosophic immunity.

SECRETARY: All right. So I take bribes. It only puts me on the same level with you.

THIRD: What!

SECOND: I smell corruption.

SIXTH: Let's hear it. Come on, out with it.

SECRETARY: You've been bought. You've all been bought.

FOURTH [*on his feet.*]: Withdraw that statement!

THIRD: Immediately.

FIRST: This has me curious. Has anyone been accepting money on my behalf? All I ask is my cut.

FOURTH: It is an unforgivable insult.

FIFTH: Let the man speak. Which of us has been taking money?

SECRETARY: Oh, not money, I know the sight of cash if printed over with INSULT for upright men like you and intellectual minds. Oh no, not cash. But position, yes, position! And the power of being so close to power, 'Well it's difficult but I'll see what I can do'. 'You understand, my private feelings cannot come into this but that's the position. Oh yes, if you think that will help, do mention the fact that I sent you.' And the dark impersonal protocol suits, and the all-purpose face, the give-nothing-away face in conference corridors, star-struck with the power of saying, 'Yes, I think I could arrange for you to meet the President.' Of

course you've been bought. Bribed with the bribe of an
all-powerful signature across a timeless detention order.
[*A brief pause.*]

FIFTH: Hm. What do you think of that, gentlemen?

THIRD: A rotten exposition.

SECRETARY: Well I never did claim to be a theoretician.

SIXTH: I confess I found it very absorbing.

FIFTH: Me too. I quite forgot my hunger for a while.

THIRD: Will you leave your stomach out of it!

SIXTH: Why does that always set you raving?

THIRD: I suffer from ulcers.

SIXTH: Don't we all? Mine are crying out for a decent meal.

THIRD: I tell you it's my ulcers.

SIXTH: I know, I know. You wait until we all break the fast on
that New Yam.

FIRST: Which we have not yet secured. Isn't it time we returned
to that subject.

FIFTH: You carry on with it. I think I'll have a word with our
Organising Secretary first. We may both find a common
ground of understanding. Come this way my friend.

SECRETARY: Kindly resume the disputations. Kongi expects an
answer soon.
[*They move to one side.*]

FIFTH: Danlola was in your charge. Kongi rightly expects that
you should have broken all his resistance by now. But you
haven't, have you?

SECRETARY: He is a stubborn ass.

FIFTH: Well, maybe. Your problem could be quite simple, only
it will have to depend on your powers of persuasion.

SECRETARY: What else do you think I've been doing all these
months.

FIFTH: Working on that wrong person. Now, before I tell you
what to do, we must settle on a fee.

SECRETARY: You . . . want me to pay you?

FIFTH: Naturally. I am a professional theoretician. I must be paid
for my services.

SECRETARY: Nothing doing.

FIFTH [*turning away*.]: In that case I shall contribute my solution to
the general pool and let my colleagues take the credit for it.

SECRETARY: Wait.

FIFTH: That's better. You can't pretend that you wouldn't be
glad to succeed where he failed.

SECRETARY: But suppose it doesn't work, this mysterious
solution of yours.

FIFTH: I can't see why it shouldn't.

SECRETARY: All right, let's hear it.

FIFTH: First, the fee.

SECRETARY: I thought you lot were supposed to be above this
sort of thing

FIFTH: You'll be surprised. Let's get back to business. I know
you're making quite a bit out of the Harvest.

SECRETARY: All right, you name your terms.

FIFTH: No, that's not the way it's usually done. You make me an
offer. And don't think I'm a novice at this game.

SECRETARY: All right. What about . . .?

[*Casually holds out a closed fist. Fifth Aweri shakes his head.*]
No? I've known contracts for a ten mile road settled for
less than. . . .
[*Two closed fists.*]
You are a hard man. Of course I must admit that the cost of
living rises all the time. My contacts in the Ministry of
Housing tell me that a modest office block was won by a
round figure close to. . . .
[*Cups his two hands together, slowly.*]
A juicy, stream-lined shape I think. . . .
[*Fifth Aweri turns his back. Secretary speaks hastily.*]
But by no means final. An artist must experiment with
shapes. I would add, by way of attraction, a pair of ears. . . .

[*He sticks out the two thumbs. Obtaining only a wooden
response, he throws up his hands angrily.*]
Well in that case take your solution where you please.
Just how much do you think I will make for myself from
organising the Harvest anyway. I may as well hand you my
entire profits.

FIFTH [*chuckling.*]: Oh I've always longed to see that done by a
professional.

SECRETARY: You would appear to be something of one yourself.

FIFTH: No, to tell you the truth, my interest has been purely
clinical.

SECRETARY: Do you mean you don't want a fee after all?

FIFTH: You bet I do. [*gives a quick look round, desperately.*]
Food man, food. A bit of the Harvest before the banquet.
I've had enough of this starvation act. Smuggle in some
food tonight.

SECRETARY: Is that all?

FIFTH: But do it carefully. Their noses are so pinched from
hunger, they will smell out any food within a two-mile
radius.

SECRETARY: Well, well. Any particular preference?

FIFTH: Yes, food. Just food.

SECRETARY: It's a deal. Now. . . .

FIFTH: My solution? Simple. Kongi is the man you have to
tackle.

SECRETARY: Please, don't try to make a fool of me.

FIFTH: I am deadly serious. Persuade him to grant some form of
amnesty. Then go to Danlola and tell him that in exchange
for the New Yam, a few of the detainees will be set free.

FIRST: And you think that will have the slightest effect on the old
man? He'll say they will be chucked right back again at the
first excuse.

FIFTH: Good. In that case, you will need something more
substantial won't you?

SECRETARY: Like what for heaven's sake?

FIFTH: Think. If Kongi were persuaded to grant a
reprieve to the men condemned to death. . . .

SECRETARY: You are out of your mind.

FIFTH: If you are able to assure Danlola that they will be
reprieved. . . .

SECRETARY: You are raving. Kongi does not want the new yam
that badly.

FIFTH: You are good at these things. Rack your brain for some
way of getting him in the right mood.

SECRETARY: You don't know how he hates those men. He wants
them dead—you've no idea how desperately.

FIFTH: I do. But tell him he can kill them later in detention.
Have them shot trying to escape or something. But first,
demonstrate his power over life and death by granting
them a last-minute reprieve. That's it, work on that aspect
of it, the drama of a last-minute reprieve. If I know my
Kongi that should appeal to his flair for gestures.

SECRETARY: It might work.

FIFTH: It will. [*going.*] And don't come back without my fee.
I can't last much longer.

Segi's Club

DAODU: Those are Segi's friends you insulted.

SECRETARY: They are not her type.

DAODU: I assure you they are.

SECRETARY: She belongs in a different class.

DAODU: She won't agree with you.

SECRETARY: What do you come to do here anyway? Are you
Segi's lover?

DAODU: Yes.

SECRETARY: I should have said, current lover.

DAODU: I *am* her current lover.

SECRETARY: There is something I don't understand. This is not the Segi we hear of. This one seemed to look at you as a woman should. The Segi we know never does.

DAODU: You keep postponing what you want to say about the Harvest.

SECRETARY: This place bothers me. I have a sixth sense about things, that is how I survive in this job. Something is missing. There should be a pungent odour of fornication about places like this. Is business slack tonight or something?

DAODU: I'll ask Segi if you like.

SECRETARY: No, no, leave her out of it. She'll confuse me. It was bad enough when I wasn't even drunk.

DAODU: Then what did you come to see me about?

SECRETARY: We closed down this quarter once didn't we?

DAODU: I don't know.

SECRETARY: Yes we did. All the prostitutes were sent off to a rehabilitation camp, and on graduation they became the Women's Auxilliary Corps, a sort of female leg of the Carpenters' Brigade.

DAODU: You must have missed out some.

SECRETARY: Oh no, we were very thorough. Make no mistake about that, we picked the kind of men for the job who would be thorough.

DAODU: Then these came after the er . . . the purge.

SECRETARY: Impossible. It couldn't have flourished so quickly.

DAODU: Why not? Some of the credit is in fact, yours. Do you mean you don't recognise any of them?

SECRETARY: What do you mean? I am not in the habit of con-sorting with. . . .

DAODU: Sit down. Take a look at that one over there . . . don't you know who she is?

SECRETARY [*looks intently, gives up.*]: She doesn't mean a thing to me.

DAODU: Go inside then. Look in the bar and in the dark corners. See if there is someone you remember.

[*As he rises, Segi comes out. He pulls himself right against a wall as if he does not want her to touch him. Segi goes past him without a glance, sits at her former table. Secretary stops suddenly, turns round and stares. Segi keeps her eyes on Daodu who in turn continues to look at the Secretary, in half-mockery. From inside, the music rises.*]

DAODU: Don't you like the music any more. They're saying—

> Your eyes were bathed
> In tender waters
> Milk of all mothers
> Flowed through your fingers
> At your hour of birth

And they say of her skin, it is a flash of *agbadu** through the sun and into cool shadows. Of her nipples, a palm nut, red flesh and black shadows, and violent as thorns.

SECRETARY: I can remember her. If I tried hard. But my brain is all addled.

DAODU:
> A coiled snake
> Is beautiful asleep
> A velvet bolster
> Laid on flowers
>
> If the snake would
> Welcome me, I do not wish
> A softer pillow than
> This lady's breasts
>
> But do not fool with one
> Whose bosom ripples
> As a python coiled
> In wait for rabbits.

*black, glistening snake

SECRETARY [*shuts his eyes tightly and holds his head.*] I know I
can remember. Isn't she the same one of whom they
warn—

> Do not stay by the sea
> At night
> Mammy Watta frolics by the sea
> At night
> Do not play
> With the Daughter of the sea. . . .

It's picking at my mind but it just will not surface.

DAODU: She is still, but only as
> The still heart of a storm.
> Segi, turn on me eyes
> That were bathed in tender seas
> And tender springs

[*The Secretary's face becomes clear suddenly, he opens his eyes,
stares hard at Segi.*]

DAODU: Your eyes are
> Cowrie shells, their cups
> Have held much brine

> It rained
> Beads of grace
> That hour of your birth

> But it fell
> From baleful skies.

SECRETARY: I am never wrong. I know now who she is. And the
rest of them. Why are they here? Is this another vigil?

DAODU: For the condemned, yes. Not for Kongi.

SECRETARY: I am not really frightened. Yours is a strangely
cheerful vigil.

DAODU: We are a cheerful lot. Moreover [*looks at his watch*] we
are expecting news.

SECRETARY: I came here with a proposal.

DAODU: Which you haven't made.

SECRETARY: If she is who I'm sure now she is, this should interest her.

DAODU: Shall I call her over?

SECRETARY: No. You can tell her afterwards—if you wish.

DAODU: Well? The proposal.

SECRETARY: Five men are awaiting execution.

DAODU: We know that.

SECRETARY: They will be reprieved—if your uncle co-operates. Think about it—I'll be back.

[*Flees, looking nervously back.*]

Kongi's Retreat
The Aweri are dozing. Kongi descends from his cell.

KONGI: I can't hear voices.

SECRETARY: I think they are meditating.

KONGI: Meditating is my province. They are here to hold disputations.

[*He looks over the partition.*]

That is no meditation. They are fast asleep!

SECRETARY [*joins him at the screen.*]: You're right. They are sleeping.

KONGI: They are always sleeping. What is the matter with them?

SECRETARY: I heard one or two of them mention hunger.

KONGI: Hunger? They are fed daily aren't they? I see to their food myself.

SECRETARY: I think they haven't got used to the diet.

KONGI: Damn their greedy guts. I eat nothing at all.

SECRETARY: Not everyone can be a Kongi.

KONGI: Strike the gong and wake them up.

[*Secretary strikes the gong, there is no response.*]

SECRETARY: They are practically dead.

KONGI: Dead? How dead? I don't remember condemning any of them to death. Or maybe I should?

SECRETARY: You still need them Leader.

KONGI: But they are sleeping.

SECRETARY: Let me try again.

[*strikes the gong.*]

I think they are really out. They've been overworking their brains I think.

KONGI: Overwork? Nonsense. They do nothing but quarrel among themselves. Every time I set them a subject for disputation they quarrel like women and then fall asleep. What do they find to quarrel about?

SECRETARY: Philosophy can be a violent subject.

KONGI: You think so? I wonder sometimes. You should have seen them during the writing of my last book. I couldn't think for the squabbles.

SECRETARY: Oh that must have been plain jealousy.

KONGI: Jealousy? Of whom are they jealous?

SECRETARY: Of one another, my Leader. You shouldn't give your books to only one person to write.

KONGI: Really? But he's the best disputant of the lot. I like his style. You shall hear the Harvest speech he's prepared for me. Four and a half hours—no joke eh?

SECRETARY: Well, it causes dissension. At least let one of the others select the title or write the footnotes.

KONGI [*pleased no end.*] Dear, dear, I had no idea they were so jealous. Very disturbing. I like harmony you realise. But I never seem to find it. And among my philosophers especially, there must be perfect harmony.

SECRETARY: Then write more books. Write enough to go round all of them.

KONGI: Oh, would that be wise? It wouldn't do to become too

prolific you know. I wouldn't want to be mistaken for a full-time author.

SECRETARY: Your duty to the country, and to the world demands far more works from you than you produce at present. Moreover, it will make your theoreticians happy.

KONGI: Hm. I think I'll trust your judgement. Tell them they can begin work on my next book as soon as the new one is released.

SECRETARY: Who is to write it my Leader?

KONGI: Let them toss for it.

[*Kongi's chant swells louder.*]

SECRETARY: Can you hear them my Leader?

KONGI: What?

SECRETARY: Your Carpenters' Brigade. They have been keeping vigil with you at the foot of the mountain.

KONGI: An inspired creation of mine don't you think?

SECRETARY: They would lay down their lives for you.

KONGI: I trust no one. They will be in attendance tomorrow?

SECRETARY: Need you ask that?

KONGI: They complement my sleepy Aweris here. These ones look after my intellectual needs, the Brigade take care of the occasional physical requirements.

SECRETARY: They will not be needed tomorrow.

KONGI: Just the same, let them stand by. Nothing must disturb the harmony of the occasion . . . ah, I like that song.

SECRETARY: It is an invocation to the Spirit of Harvest to lend you strength.

KONGI [*violently.*]: I *am* the Spirit of Harvest.

[*The Aweri stir.*]

SECRETARY: S-sh. They are waking up.

KONGI [*alarmed, looks round wildly.*]: Who? The people?

[*Recovers slowly, angrily begins to climb the steps leading to his cell. Secretary follows him, appeasing.*]

KONGI: I *am* the Spirit of Harvest.

SECRETARY: Of course my Leader, the matter is not in dispute.

KONGI: I am the SPIRIT of Harvest.

SECRETARY: Of course my Leader.

KONGI: I am the Spirit of HAAR-VEST!

SECRETARY: Of course my Leader. And a benevolent Spirit of Harvest. This year shall be known as the year of Kongi's Harvest. Everything shall date from it.

KONGI [*stops suddenly.*]: Who thought that up?

SECRETARY: It is among the surprise gifts we have planned for our beloved Leader. I shouldn't have let it slip out. . . .

KONGI [*rapt in the idea.*]: You mean, things like 200 K.H.

SECRETARY: A.H. my Leader. After the Harvest. In a thousand years, one thousand A.H. And last year shall be referred to as 1 B.H. There will only be the one Harvest worth remembering.

KONGI: No, K.H. is less ambiguous. The year of Kongi's Harvest. Then for the purpose of back-dating, B.K.H. Before Kongi's Harvest. No reason why we should conform to the habit of two initials only. You lack imagination.

SECRETARY: It shall be as you please my Leader.

KONGI: Now you see why it is all the more important that everything goes forward tomorrow as I wish it? I want the entire nation to subscribe to it. Wake up those hogs!

SECRETARY: It isn't necessary my Leader. I think the little problem of Danlola is nearly solved.

KONGI: Another of your ideas?

SECRETARY: Leave it all to me. I er . . . oh yes, I ought to mention one other matter. I . . . have reason to believe that a press photographer might find his way into your retreat in spite of all our precautions for your privacy. [*Enter photographer.*]

KONGI: Oh dear, you know I wouldn't like that at all. [*He strikes a pose of anguish, camera clicks.*]

SECRETARY: In fact we think we know who it is. A foreign
    journalist, one of the best. He plans to leak it to a chain of
    foreign newspapers under the caption—Last Day of
    Meditation; A Leader's Anguish! I have seen some of his
    work, the work of a genius. He has photographed at least
    nine heads of state.

KONGI: I wouldn't like it at all.

SECRETARY: If we catch him we shall expel him at once.

KONGI: No, after the Harvest.

SECRETARY: Of course after the Harvest. The Leader's place of
    meditation should be sancrosanct.

    [*Moves to an opening, and poses his best profile.*]

KONGI: Twilight gives the best effect—of course I speak as an
    amateur.

    [*Click.*]

SECRETARY: But you are right. I have noticed its mystical aura
    in the mountains. I think our man is bound to come at
    twilight.

KONGI: I don't like being photographed.

SECRETARY: I'll ensure it never happens again.

KONGI: Take care of it and let me hear no more on the subject.
    Some of these journalists are remarkably enterprising.
    Nothing you do can stop them.

    [*Returns to his table and goes through a series of 'Last Supper'
    poses—iyan (pounded yam) serving variation—while the
    photographer takes picture after picture.*]

SECRETARY: Yes my Leader.

KONGI: Then go and look after everything. . . . What's the
    matter? Is there anything else?

SECRETARY: Only the question of amnesty my Leader.

KONGI: Oh, I leave that to you. Release all those who have
    served their court sentences.

SECRETARY: Too trivial a gesture my Leader. Too trivial for one
    who holds the power of life and death.

KONGI [*suddenly wary.*]: What do you have in mind exactly?

SECRETARY: The men awaiting execution.

KONGI: I thought so. Who put you up to it.

SECRETARY: Another of my ideas.

KONGI: I like the ones that went before. But not this one.

SECRETARY: It's all part of one and same harmonious idea my
Leader. A Leader's Temptation. . . . Agony on the
Mountains. . . . The loneliness of the Pure. . . . The Uneasy
Head. . . . A Saint at Twilight. . . . The Spirit of the
Harvest. . . . The Face of Benevolence. . . . The Giver of
Life . . . who knows how many other titles will accompany
such pictures round the world. And then my Leader, this
is the Year of Kongi's Harvest! The Presiding Spirit as a
life-giving spirit—we could project that image into every
heart and head, no matter how stubborn.
[*As the Secretary calls each shot, Kongi poses it and the photographer shoots, bows and departs.*]

KONGI: But those men. . . .

SECRETARY: A life-giving Spirit of Harvest, by restoring life,
increasing the man-power for the Five-Year Development
Plan . . . I could do anything with that image.

KONGI: Hm.

SECRETARY: Such a gesture would even break the back of the
opposition. A contemptuous gift of life would prove that
their menace is not worth your punishment.

KONGI: Tell you what. You get all the leaders of the dissident
groups to appear on the dais with me tomorrow—all of
them, and at their head, that wretched king himself and
his entire court, bearing the new yam in his hands. Right?
You get him to do that. Him at the head of all the opposing
factions. Well? Is there anything else?

SECRETARY: But my Leader, you haven't completed the message.

KONGI: What more do you want? I say I want a total, absolute
submission—in full view of the people.

SECRETARY: And of the world press—haven't I promised it my
    Leader?

KONGI: Then get on with it. There isn't much time left you
    know.

SECRETARY: But the reprieve. You said nothing of that.

KONGI: Didn't I? Oh, all right. Tell your Danlola I'll reprieve
    those men if he co-operates fully. Now go.

SECRETARY: Leader, my magnanimous Leader!

KONGI: But look here, we must make it a last-minute reprieve.
    It will look better that way don't you think? Kongi's act
    of clemency remains a confidential decision until a quarter
    of an hour before the hanging—no, five minutes. That's
    enough of a safety margin isn't it? It had better be!

SECRETARY: It will do my Leader.

KONGI: So keep it under until then. Now go.

    [*Secretary runs off. Kongi stands for a moment, sunk in a new
    pose, thoughtful. Seizes the iron bar suddenly and strikes the
    gong. Strides among the startled Aweri.*]

KONGI: Dispute me whether it is politic to grant reprieves to the
    five men awaiting execution. And DISPUTE you hear! I
    shall go and meditate upon it.

Segi's Club

SECRETARY: Well?

DAODU: This is a certainty?

SECRETARY: I have Kongi's word. Now I want your Uncle's
    word that he will co-operate with us.

DAODU: I shall obtain it. On those conditions, he cannot
    refuse me.

SECRETARY: And no one need lose face over it.

    [*He is once more expansive, calls for beer.*]

    Who really cares for the Festival of New Yam anyway?

It is all a matter of face. The struggle began, involved
others, and no one dared give ground for the very
stink of face. But I have devised a clean solution.

DAODU: The New Yam for the lives of five men. It's a generous
bargain.

SECRETARY: Four men. One is dead, hanged himself by the belt.
Heard about it on my way here. Publicly, we shall give it
out that, as part of the Harvest amnesty, the government
has been pleased to release Oba Danlola and a few others,
then, as a gesture of reciprocity—the exact words of my
official release—as a gesture of reciprocity—the Oba will
voluntarily surrender the first yam.

DAODU: The enactment of it alone should appeal to him.
Kabiyesi loves to act roles. Like kingship. For him,
kingship is a role.

SECRETARY: Now where did I hear that before? Seems I heard
it . . . that's right. Now that's funny isn't it? One of the
Aweri said exactly the same thing of Kongi. 'A flair for
gestures' he said.

DAODU: Maybe that's why they hate each other's guts.

SECRETARY: Professional jealousy eh? Ha, ha, couldn't agree with
you more. Well then I'll take Kongi, and you deal with
your uncle. I can count on you?

DAODU: As an ally. I shall see him tonight—you will make the
arrangements?

SECRETARY: Go and see him now; you'll be admitted. Let him
know that the lives of four men hang on his decision.

DAODU: He won't refuse me.

SECRETARY: I must go now. I have to tell Kongi all is well.

DAODU: I thought he was meditating in the mountains.

SECRETARY: I am allowed to go up and see him—on urgent
state matters of course.

DAODU: Of course.

[*Secretary goes, looks round, looks off into the club.*]

SECRETARY: Where are those fools gone? [*to a waiter.*] You.
    Call me those two creatures I came in with.
    [*The waiter, a couple of the layabouts move as if to cut off his
    retreat, quietly menacing.*]

DAODU: I think they are gone.

SECRETARY: Gone? Where? I didn't see them leave.

DAODU: They shouldn't have come here.

SECRETARY: As servants of the state they can go anywhere.
    Anywhere!

DAODU: Too many people remember them. They shouldn't
    have come here.

SECRETARY [*looks round fearfully.*]: What are you trying to say?
    I thought we were allies.

DAODU: So we are. I have promised you my Uncle's public
    submission.

SECRETARY: What happened to my Ears of State?

DAODU: You forget. I'm only a farmer. I don't run this place.

SECRETARY: Well who does?

DAODU [*points.*]: Over there. Ask her.
    [*Secretary stares at her, experiencing fear. Segi rises, comes
    forward slowly.*]

SECRETARY: Your witch! What have you done to them?

DAODU: This is Segi. Once she said to herself, this man's lust,
    I'll smother it with my beauty.

SECRETARY: Lust?

DAODU: For power.

SEGI: Surely you must know me.

SECRETARY: Kongi's mystery woman. You couldn't be
    anybody else.

SEGI: Why did you come here?

SECRETARY: A mistake. Just call me the Ears of State and I'll
    leave.

SEGI: They have already left.

SECRETARY: When? Why?

DAODU: They left with Segi's friends.

SECRETARY [*sits down, dog-tired.*]: Oh! yes, it's all clear now.
Your father . . . one of the condemned men.

SEGI: You understand.

SECRETARY: I suppose this means, I am also your prisoner?

DAODU: No, ally.

SECRETARY: In that case . . . I don't wish to remain here.

DAODU: I'll see you out.

[*The layabouts look questioningly at Segi who engages in a silent
duel with Daodu. Daodu firmly takes the Secretary by the arm
and moves forward. The men make way. Segi is obviously
angry, and turns away.*]

SECRETARY: Don't forget my mission.

DAODU: I won't. You understand, your men had to go with
others—for safety. Naturally we were suspicious.

SECRETARY: No, no. I've been trying to get those men
reprieved.

DAODU: I'll take your message to Oba Danlola.

SECRETARY: My . . . bargaining position is somewhat weaker. . . .
When I left Kongi I had five lives. Then they told me one
had hanged himself. And now . . . I suppose by now her
father has escaped?

DAODU: An hour ago.

SECRETARY: That leaves me only three.

DAODU: It's enough to bargain with, for a New Yam.

SECRETARY: I'm glad you think so. I'll see you at the feast.

[*He slouches off, a heavy pathetic figure. Daodu turns to meet
Segi, smiles to break her anger.*]

DAODU: My eyes of rain, Queen of the Harvest night.

SEGI [*slowly relenting, half ashamed.*]: I was so afraid.

DAODU: There is nothing more to fear.

SEGI: I will never be afraid again.

DAODU: Two less for Kongi's grim collection. I am glad the
live one is your father.

SEGI: I feel like dancing naked. If I could again believe I would say it was a sign from heaven.

DAODU: Yes, if I were awaiting a sign, this would be it. It may turn me superstitious yet.

SEGI: I want to dance on *gbegbe* leaves; I know now I have not been forgotten.

DAODU: I'll rub your skin in camwood, you'll be flames at the hide of night.

SEGI: Come with me Daodu.

DAODU: Now? There is still much to do before you meet us at the gates.

SEGI: Come through the gates tonight. Now. I want you in me, my Spirit of Harvest.

DAODU: Don't tempt me so hard. I am swollen like prize yam under earth, but all harvest must await its season.

SEGI: There is no season for seeds bursting.

DAODU: My eyes of kernels, I have much preparation to make.

SEGI: I shall help you.

DAODU: Segi, between now and tomorrow's eve, I must somehow obtain some rest.

SEGI: Let me tire you a little more.

DAODU: You cannot know how weary I am. . . . A child could sneeze me off my legs with a little pepper.

SEGI: I must rejoice, and you with me. I am opened tonight. I am soil from the final rains.

DAODU: Promise you won't keep me long. I still have to meet my troublesome king.

SEGI: Only a bite, of your Ismite.

DAODU: Only a bite?

SEGI: Only a mite.

DAODU: Oh Segi! I had thought tonight at least, I would keep my head. [*Enter two women, bearing an unfinished robe.*]

SEGI: Ah, you must try this on before we go. It isn't finished yet but it will be ready for you tomorrow.

DAODU: This!

SEGI: They'll work on it all night if necessary.

DAODU: I didn't mean that, but . . . must I really wear this?

SEGI: Stand still!

[*They drape the robe round him.*]

DAODU: In the name of everything, what am I supposed to be?

SEGI: The Spirit of Harvest.

DAODU: I feel like the prince of orgies, I feel like some decadent deity.

SEGI: Well, that's the idea.

DAODU: Can't something simpler do?

SEGI: No. Now stand still. Be solemn for a moment.

[*She comes round, surveys him. Suddenly she kneels and clings to the hem of his robes. The other women kneel too.*]

My prince . . . my prince. . . .

DAODU: Let me preach hatred Segi. If I preached hatred I could match his barren marathon, hour for hour, torrent for torrent. . . .

SEGI: Preach life Daodu, only life. . . .

DAODU: Imprecations then, curses on all inventors of agonies, on all Messiahs of pain and false burdens. . . .

SEGI: Only life is worth preaching my prince.

DAODU [*with mounting passion.*]: On all who fashion chains, on farmers of terror, on builders of walls, on all who guard against the night but breed darkness by day, on all whose feet are heavy and yet stand upon the world. . . .

SEGI: Life . . . life. . . .

DAODU: On all who see, not with the eyes of the dead, but with eyes of Death. . . .

SEGI: Life then. It needs a sermon on life . . . love. . . .

DAODU [*with violent anger.*]: Love? Love? You who gave love, how were you requited?

SEGI [*rises.*]: My eyes were open to what I did. Kongi *was* a great man, and I loved him.

DAODU: What will I say then? What can one say on life against the batteries and the microphones and the insistence of one indefatigable madman? What is there strong enough about just living and loving? What!

SEGI: It will be enough that you erect a pulpit against him, even for one moment.

DAODU [*resignedly*.]: I hate to be a mere antithesis to your Messiah of Pain.

[*Segi begins to disrobe him. The women go off with the garment.*

The song in the background comes up more clearly—a dirge.]

DAODU: Do they all know where they may be tomorrow, by this time?

SEGI: You shouldn't worry about my women. They accepted it long ago.

DAODU: My men also. They have waited a long time for this.

SEGI: This, the last night is mine by right. Ours.

DAODU: Ours. Suddenly I have lost my tiredness. First let me go and speak with my awkward king, then I'll come back to you. [*going.*]

SEGI: Shall I stop the wake—since there is to be a reprieve?

DAODU: No, let it continue. I find grief sharpens my appetite for living.

SEGI: And loving? Come back quickly Daodu, I'll be waiting.

[*Daodu goes off; the dirge rises. All lights come on for the next scene. There is no break.*]

Kongi's retreat
Kongi shaking with anger, the Secretary cowering before him.

KONGI: Escaped?

SECRETARY: Not from my camp my Leader. It wasn't from my camp.

KONGI: Escaped? Escaped?

SECRETARY: Only one, sir. The other hanged himself.

KONGI: I want him back. I want him back you hear?

SECRETARY: He shall be caught my Leader.

KONGI: I want him back—alive if possible. If not, ANY OTHER
WAY! But I want him back!

SECRETARY: It shall be done at once my Leader.

KONGI: Get out! GO AND BRING HIM BACK!

[*Secretary turns to escape.*]

And hear this! The amnesty is OFF! The reprieve is OFF!
The others hang tomorrow.

SECRETARY: My Leader, your promise!

KONGI: No Amnesty! No Reprieve! Hang every one of them!
Hang them!

SECRETARY: Your promise my Leader. The word of Kongi!

KONGI: And find me the other one for hanging—GET OUT!
GET OUT! GET . . . AH . . . AH . . . AH . . . .

[*His mouth hanging open, from gasps into spasms and violent
convulsions, Kongi goes into an epileptic fit. Over his struggle
for breath rises Kongi's chant.*]

Second Part

*Oba Danlola's palace. Plenty of bustle and activity as if a great
preparation were in progress. Danlola is trying out one thing, rejecting
it and trying on another.*

DANLOLA: Oh, what a home-coming this is!
    I obtained much better service
    In the Detention Camp.
DENDE: But you did order a sceptre Kabiyesi.
DANLOLA: Do you dare call this a sceptre?
    This dung-stained goat prod, this
    Makeshift sign at crossroads, this
    Thighbone of the crow that died
    Of rickets? Or did you merely
    Steal the warped backscratcher
    Of your hunchback uncle?
DENDE: I got no co-operation at all
    From the blacksmith. It was the best
    I found in the blacksmith's foundry.
DANLOLA: Some soup-pot foundry. Find me
    Such another ladle and I'll
    Shove it up your mother's fundaments.
DAODU [*storms in. Stops short as he sees signs of activity.*]: I was
    told you would not take part in today's procession.
DANLOLA: The ostrich also sports plumes but
    I've yet to see that wise bird
    Leave the ground.
DAODU: But all this preparation. . . .
DANLOLA: When the dog hides a bone does he not
    Throw up sand? A little dust in the eye

Of His Immortality will not deceive
His clever Organising Secretary. We need to
Bury him in shovelfuls.
[*Re-enter Dende.*]
You horse manure! Is this a trip
To gather mangoes for the hawker's tray?
Tell me, did I ask for a basket fit
To support your father's goitre? I thought
I specially designed a copper salver.

DENDE: The smith had done nothing at all
About it.

DANLOLA: The smith! The smith! All I hear
Is of some furnace blower called
The smith!

DAODU [*sharply, to Dende.*]: Send for the Smith.

DANLOLA: I have more important preparations
Than to break wind with the smith.
Take that thing right back to where
It was aborted from, and tell him
I want my copper salver.

DENDE: Copper, Kabiyesi?

DANLOLA: Copper yes. Copper the colour of earth
In harvest. Do you think I'll serve the first
Of our New Yam in anything but copper?

DAODU: Since you don't intend to be present anyway, why
all this energy?

DANLOLA: The Big Ear of the Man Himself
Has knocked twice on my palace gates—
Twice in one morning—and his spies
Have sneaked in through the broken wall
Of my backyard, where women throw their piss
As many times today.

DAODU: And why does he suspect you?

DANLOLA: I have, dear son, a reputation for

       Falling ill on these state occasions.
       And, to tell the truth, they make me
       Ill. So my friends the Eyes and Ears
       Of State set prying fingers to sieve
       My chamber pot, diagnose my health,
       And analyse every gesture.

DAODU: Isn't it much simpler to go? After all you did
       promise. . . .

DANLOLA: I promised nothing that I will not
       Fulfil.

DAODU: You gave your word.

DANLOLA: Indeed I gave my word and if you like
       I swear again to exhaust your eyes and ears
       With that word undergoing fulfilment.

DAODU: You should go. It's a small thing to sacrifice—
       I thought we agreed on that and you gave your word.

DANLOLA: You should, my son, when you deal in politics
       Pay sharp attention to the word. I agreed
       Only that I would prepare myself
       For the grand ceremony, not
       That I would go. Hence this bee hum fit
       For the world's ruling heads jammed
       In annual congress. When my servants
       Are later questioned, they'll bear witness
       How I set the royal craftsmen slaving
       At such short notice to make me ready
       To present the New Yam to my Leader.

DAODU: How do you expect him—them—to take your absence?

DANLOLA: As an act of God. Perhaps I'll be
       Smitten with a heart attack from
       My loyal efforts. Or it could be
       The Oracle forbade me budging from
       My chamber walls today. As the Man
       Himself has often screamed, we are

A backward superstitious lot, immune
To Kongi's adult education schemes.

DAODU: I should have believed it. I was warned you might go
back on your word.

DANLOLA: Now where could you have picked that up?
In those dives of *tombo* where you pass
The hours of sleep?

DAODU: I see it's not Kongi's men alone who have an efficient
spy system.

DANLOLA: For us, even the dead lend their eyes
And ears, as do also the unborn.

DAODU: But you find something wrong with the eyes of the
living?

DANLOLA: They are the eyes of fear. But tell me,
How is the woman?

DAODU: Who?

DANLOLA: Who? Are you playing lawyer to
Oba Danlola, the Ears of wind and dry
Maize leaves? I asked, how fares
The woman whose eyes unblinking as
The eyes of the dead have made you drunk?

DAODU: I don't know what woman you mean.

DANLOLA [*bursts suddenly into laughter.*]:
They say you can always tell the top
By the way it dances. If anyone had doubts
Whose son you are, you've proved you are
No bastard. A-ah, you have picked yourself
A right cannibal of the female species.

DAODU: I think I'll go on to watch the procession. . . .

DANLOLA: Stay where you are! Tell me, do you
Know that woman's history? I have myself
Wandered round some dens of Esu, once,
And clambered over sweet hillocks
In the dark, and not missed my way. But

Daodu, that woman of yours, she scares
The pepper right up the nostrils
Of your old man here. She has left victims
On her path like sugar cane pulp
Squeezed dry.

DAODU: Men know nothing of Segi. They only sing songs
about her.

DANLOLA: Much better not to know, believe your father.
Oh you have chosen to be swallowed whole
Down the oyster throat of the witch
Of night clubs. Segi! Son, she'll shave
Your skull and lubricate it in oil.
[*Enter Dende.*]

DENDE: Kabiyesi ... about the er—your royal canopy.

DANLOLA: Well—is it ready at last?

DENDE: No sir. Er—it seems
The snake-skins have all been used up.

DANLOLA: Then use the one you moulted
Yesterday, you single-gut
Hunter of toads!
[*Enter Secretary.*]
Ah, you were surely
Summoned by my head. You see yourself
How the courtesan is one hour escalating
Her brocade head-tie, and the devil-wind
Whisks it out of sight just when the sun
Has joined to make it dazzle men

SECRETARY: Kabiyesi, what is the matter?

DANLOLA: The matter? The things they bring me
Anyone would think I was headed
For a pauper's funeral.

SECRETARY: But you will be late. The things you have on you
will do just as well.

DANLOLA: What! These trimmings may serve

A wayside lunatic, but my friend,
We must meet the Leader as
A conquering hero, not welcome him
Like some corner-corner son-in-law.

DENDE [*enters.*]: Perhaps you would prefer this Kabiyesi.
It belonged to my great
Grandfather on my mother's side. . . .

DANLOLA: Oh, what a joy you must have been
To your great progenitors until
They died of overjoy! The Leader
Visits us today—is that not enough?
Must I ask him also to make a sword
Of state, fit to grace his presence?

SECRETARY: All this is quite unnecessary Kabiyesi. We appreciate
your zeal and I assure you it will not go unmentioned.
But it is your presence our Leader requires. . . .

DANLOLA: You wish to make me a laughing-stock?

SECRETARY: You know how we deal with those who dare make
fun of the Leader's favoured men.

DANLOLA: Then, my dear son-in-politics, this being
The only way in which our dignity
May be retained without the risk
Of conflict with the new authority,
Let us be seen in public only as
Befits our state. Not to add the fact
That this is Harvest. An Oba must emerge
In sun colours as a laden altar.

SECRETARY: Kabiyesi, I don't suggest for a moment that. . . .

DANLOLA: I know we are the masquerade without
Flesh or spirit substance, but we can
Afford the best silk on our government
Pension. Now you! Tell the smith he must
Produce the sword I ordered specially.

DENDE: He says that would require at least. . . .

DANLOLA: Enough, enough, I'll use this as it is
Get a new cover on it, some tit-bit
Of leather—and don't tell me you have
No left-over scraps enough to hide
A rusty scabbard. I know your pumice
Stomach can digest it. Move!
A-ah, my good Organising Secretary of
His Immortality our Kongi, you see
What agonies these simple ceremonies
Demand of us?

SECRETARY: You really haven't that much time you
know. It would be simpler....

DANLOLA: You haven't met my heir have you?
Lately returned from everywhere and still
Trying to find his feet. Not surprisingly.
It must be hard to find one's feet in such
Thin arrowheads. Daodu, before you
Flaps the Big Ear of his Immortality.
Make friends with him. Your decaying
Father is most deeply in his debt.
In these trying times, it is good to know
The Big Ear of his government.

SECRETARY: Your Uncle is a most difficult man.

DANLOLA: Difficult? Me difficult? Why should
A father be difficult and obstruct
His children's progress? No, I have told you
Listen less to those who carry tales
From sheer envy.

SECRETARY [*to Daodu.*]: What is he up to?
[*Danlola pricks up his ears.*]

DAODU: I'm not sure. I am still feeling the ground.

DANLOLA: You'll feel the ground until
It gives way under you. What
I ask you, is there to feel?

Oh, never mind, I suppose it gives
You children pleasure to pretend
There are new cunnings left for
The world to discover . . . Dende!

DENDE [*runs in.*]: Kabiyesi.

DANLOLA: Dende, do you realise you keep
A whole nation waiting?

DENDE: Kabiyesi, you asked me to stuff
The Crown with cotton.

DANLOLA: Ah, so I did. Age has shrunk
The tortoise and the shell is full
Of air pockets. My head
Now dances in my crown like a colanut
In the pouch of an *ikori* cap.
Well, why do you stand there? Waiting
Still for the cotton fall of the next
Harmattan?
[*Dende runs off.*]

SECRETARY: Couldn't you manage it at all? We are really
short of time.

DANLOLA: Manage it? Will there not be six times
At the least when we must up and bow
To Kongi? These are no bones
To rush an old man after a crown
That falls off his head and rolls
Into a gutter.
[*Royal drums heard in distance.*]

SECRETARY: I will have to leave you. The other Obas are already
arriving. Someone has to be there to group each entourage
in their place.

DANLOLA: You must hurry or the confusion
Will be worse than shoes before the
Praying-ground at Greater Beiram.

SECRETARY: Kabiyesi, please follow quickly. It will make my

task easier if I can get all the Obas settled before our
Leader arrives.
[*Enter Dende.*]

DANLOLA: No, not that one! Is that a crown
　　　To wear on such a day?

DENDE: But I took it from. . . .

DANLOLA: The same dunghill you use for pillow!

DENDE: But Kabiyesi, this is your favourite
　　　Crown. It belonged to Kadiri, the great
　　　Ancestor warrior of your lineage.

DANLOLA: Who rests in peace we pray. And now
　　　My pious wish is—burn it! Burn it
　　　With firewood from the dessicated trunk
　　　Of your family tree.

SECRETARY [*stares, speechless and turns in desperation to
　　　Daodu.*]:
　　　Are you coming to the square?

DAODU: Oh I don't really know.

DANLOLA: He never really knows, that thoughtful
　　　Son of mine. Go with the man. If anyone
　　　Can conjure you a seat close to the Great
　　　Visitor himself, he can.

SECRETARY: Yes, I was going to suggest that. Why don't you
　　　come now? I'm sure I can squeeze you in somewhere.

DAODU: In a minute.

SECRETARY: Good. Kabiyesi, we shall expect you.
　　　[*he goes.*]

DANLOLA: And I, you. But here, within
　　　My audience chambers. I have done enough
　　　Of this play-acting.
　　　[*Begins leisurely to remove his trappings. Drums, bugles etc.
　　　announce the approach of Oba Sarumi and retinue
　　　Dende rushes in.*]

DENDE: Kabiyesi, Oba Sarumi is at the palace gates.

DANLOLA: Let him enter. I suppose he wants
    Our four feet to dance together
    To the meeting-place.

PRAISE-SINGER: [*leads in, singing.*]:
    E ma gun' yan Oba kere o   Don't pound the king's yam
    E ma gun' yan Oba kere   In a small mortar
    [*Enter Sarumi, prostrates himself.*]

DANLOLA: Get up, get up man. An Oba Grade I
    By the grace of Chieftaincy Succession
    Legislation Section II, nineteen-twenty-one
    Demands of you, not this lizard posture
    But a mere governmental bow—from
    The waist, if you still have one.

SARUMI [*joining the singer.*]:   Don't pound the king's yam
    E ma gun' yan Oba kere o   In a small mortar
    E ma gun' yan Oba kere   Small as the spice is
    Kaun elepini o se gbe mi   It cannot be swallowed whole
    Eweyo noin ni i fi yo'nu   A shilling's vegetable must appease
    Ema gun' yan Oba kere   A halfpenny spice

DANLOLA: Go and tell that to the Leader's men
    Their yam is pounded, not with the pestle
    But with stamp and a pad of violet ink
    And their arms make omelet of
    Stubborn heads, via police truncheons.

SARUMI: The king is
    Oba ni if'itan ebo ha'yin   He who chews on the haunch from an
    Orisa'oba   The king is a god   [offering

DANLOLA: At least get up from that position
    Sit down and go easy on my eyes.
    I can't look down without my glasses.

SARUMI [*rises, still singing.*]:   The king is
    He who anoints the head's pulse centre
    Oba ni if'epo inv ebo r'awuje   With the oil of sacrifice
    Orisa l'oba.   The king is a god

DANLOLA: *Orisa l'oba*? Hadn't you better see
The new *orisa* in the market square
Before you earn yourself a lock-up
For reactionary statements.

SARUMI: Kabiyesi, your voice was the dawn pigeon
Which summoned us from drowsy mats
We do not know the jackal's call
We do not hear the bonded overseer
When the father speaks.

DANLOLA: Wise birdlings learn to separate
The pigeon's cooing from the shrill alarm
When Ogun stalks the forests.

SARUMI: The boldest hunter knows when
The gun must be unspiked. When a squirrel
Seeks sanctuary up the *iroko* tree
The hunter's chase is ended. . . .
In Oba Danlola's palace his sons
Speak out their minds. [*dances.*]

PRAISE-SINGER: Ogun did not seek the throne
  Ogun o l'oun o j'oba   Ogun did not seek the throne
  Ogun o l'oun o j'oba   Quietly retired, minding his own business
  Jeje l'Ogun se jeje   The nobles brought the crown of Ire
  T'ijoye gb'ade Ire wa be baba To the ancestor of all hunters
  Ogun o l'oun o j'oba   [*ode* Ogun did not seek the throne

DANLOLA: You'll be more at home performing
At the Festival of Traditional Arts

SARUMI: *Ma binu simi Oba.* . . .

DANLOLA: Look, if you want to please me, dip
in your regal pouch and find me
Some colanut. Playing a clown's part
For the Eye and Ear of his Immortality
Has turned my blood to water. I need
The stain of cola to revive
Its royal stain.

SARUMI [*gives him cola.*]:   White nut from the offering
   Orogbo ebo, awuje Oba. . . .   Pulse of the Oba's head

DANLOLA: Don't tell me this is colanut
   From a wayside bowl! Dende!
DENDE [*rushes in.*]: Kabiyesi.
DANLOLA: Bring the schnapps. Esu alone knows
   Where this colanut was picked. Not that
   It matters. The schnapps should take
   Good care of sacrificial germs. I suppose
   After all your exercise, some schnapps
   Would come in handy too.
   [*Sarumi's dance grows positively ecstatic, Daodu remains
   intensely frustrated but undecided.*]

SARUMI:

   Ma ma binu si mi Oba   Be not angry my king with me
   B'esumare se binu si'takun   As the rainbow, full of wrath at the root
   To ta kete, to ta kete   Drew away, pulled apart
   To ran'ri s'agbede meji orun And settled half-way to heaven

   Ma binu simi Oba   Be not angry my king with me   [earth
   Bi Sango se binu s'araiye.   As Sango was angered by the people of
   To di pe manamana ni i fi   Till only with the language of lightning
   Mba omo enia soro   Does he now hold converse with man

   Ma binu si mi Oba   Be not angry with me my king   [tapper
   B'iwin ope se binu s'elemu   As the palm ghommid, in anger at the wine-
   To re alangba lu'le   Plucked the lizard down to earth
   Bi eni ha kuruna l'ori   As a man scratches scabs from his head

   [*Danlola begins slowly to glow, to expand, to be visibly affected
   by the praise-singing.*]

   Oba o se e te   The king is not for treading on
   Bi eni te r'awe   As a man steps on dried leaves
   B'ajanaku o rora rin   If the elephant does not warily step
   A t'egun mole   He will tread on a thorn
   A d'atiro tiro tiro   And hobble like a pair of stilts

K.H.—3

Oba o se e gbon	The king is not to be shaken off
Bi eni gbon t'akun	As a man may brush off cobwebs
Igbon oba, awon eru	A king's beard is an awesome net
Ogbon oba, iwon eru	A king's wisdom is awesome measure
Esin to r'ebo ti o sare	Whatever fly cuts a careless caper
Tin nta felefele	Around the scent of sacrifice
Enu alantakun ni o bo.	Will worship down the spider's throat.

[*Danlola, totally swelled, steps down from his throne and falls
in step with Sarumi. The two Obas cavort round the chamber in
sedate, regal steps and the bugles blasts a steady refrain.
Danlola's wives emerge and join in; the atmosphere is full of
the ecstasy of the dance. At its height Daodu moves with sudden
decision, pulls out the ceremonial whisk of Danlola and hits the
lead drum with the heavy handle. It bursts. There is a dead
silence. Danlola and Daodu face each other in a long, terrible
silence.*]

SARUMI [*in a horrified whisper.*]: *Efun!*

DANLOLA [*shakes his head slowly.*]:
　　No. Your son has his senses
　　Intact. He must know what he is doing.

SARUMI: *Efun! Efun!* Someone has done this to him. Some
　　enemy has put a curse on my first-born.

DANLOLA [*climbing back to his throne, wearily.*]:
　　Life gets more final every day. That prison
　　Superintendent merely lay his hands
　　On my lead drummer, and stopped
　　The singing, but you our son and heir
　　You've seen to the song itself.

DAODU: Kabiyesi . . .

DANLOLA: It is a long long time my limbs
　　Rejoiced that way. I swear a snake
　　Ran wildly through my veins and left

Its moulting in my train. . . . A-ah
Matters will go hard upon
A royal favourite tonight. I feel
Life resurrected within me and I
Shall resurrect my dance on softer springing
Than this dung-baked floor. In fact
To confess the truth, I doubt
If matters can await the dark.
Call me that Dende.

DAODU: I only want a few words. . . .

DANLOLA: I know the drums were silenced long
Before you, but you have split
The gut of our make-believe. Suddenly
The world has run amok and left you
Alone and sane behind

DAODU: In that case, you know I have a reason.

DANLOLA: And I do not choose to hear it.
When the next-in-line claps his hand
Over a monarch's mouth, it is time
For him to take to the final sleep
Or take to drink and women.

DAODU: It is vital that you hand the Leader what he wants.
I cannot explain it now. Time is short and we have
much to do. But I must have your word that you will play
your part.

DANLOLA: Make my excuses to him—my son-in-politics
Will help you. Tell his Immortality
I sprained my back rehearsing dances
In honour of his visit. He loves to see
His Obas prancing to amuse him after all
And excess zeal should be a credit.

DAODU: I have no thoughts of Kongi. This matter concerns us,
your children. Don't ask me to say more—I cannot now.
I dare not. Kabiyesi, this is no time for trivialities. We shall

all have our dance tonight, when it matters, and I
promise you the event will make its own amends.

DANLOLA: I wish you luck. Dende!
Where on earth is that fool!
I am not young like you, and these
Sudden surges must be canalised.
Who knows? There may be another son
From this, if so, rest assured
I'll name him after you—to mark
This morning's work.

DAODU: You swore to me. Early this morning you
swore to me.

DANLOLA [*with sudden unexpected anger.*]:
And so, you child, did Kongi.
Did he not promise a reprieve
For the condemned men, in return
For the final act of my humiliation?
Well, did he not?

DAODU: Yes, and I know our man will remind him of it.

DANLOLA: Then perhaps you have not heard
What the wooden box announced
As I returned to palace. Such a welcoming
I've never known. Did not one
Of the dying enemies of Kongi
Seize suddenly on life by jumping
Through the prison walls?

DAODU: I heard about it.

DANLOLA: And the radio has put out a price
Upon his head. A life pension
For his body, dead or alive. That
Dear child, is a new way to grant
Reprieves. Alive, the radio blared,
If possible; and if not—DEAD!
I didn't say it, the radio did

In my primitive youth, that would be called
A plain incitement to murder.

DAODU: It means nothing. Nothing can alter what today will
bring. And your compliance is a vital part of it.

DANLOLA: My vital part shall exhaust itself
In my favourite's bed. Call me Wuraola.
Go hand Kongi the New Yam yourself
But count me out

SARUMI: Kabiyesi, age is nectar
May the royal household ever
Savour its blessings.

DANLOLA: Take your son with you,
Prepare him for my crown and beads
This king is done.

SARUMI: Kabiyesi, live long, reign long and peaceful. Our line
does not seek this kind of succession which bears a silent
curse. I know my son has something for old ears like ours.
You have to listen.

DANLOLA: Out of my way.

DAODU [*desperately.*]: The woman you warned me about, Segi,
the witch of night clubs as you labelled her, is the daughter
of this man who has escaped. And she wants the Harvest
to go on as we all planned, as much as I.
[*Danlola turns slowly round.*]

DANLOLA: Is this the truth about that woman?

DAODU: The truth.

DANLOLA [*hesitates and a far-seeing look comes into his eyes.*]:
There was always something more, I knew
To that strange woman beyond
Her power to turn grown men to infants.
[*He looks long and kindly at Daodu, then incredulous.*]:
And this woman, you say
Her father is already free, and yet
She wants the Harvest to be held

As ... planned?

DAODU: She does.

DANLOLA: And what Harvest do you children
    Mean to give the world?

DAODU: Kabiyesi, is it not you elders who say ...?

DANLOLA: The eyes of divination never close
    But whoever boasts Ifa greeted him
    With open lips ... well, so be it. Sarumi,
    It seems our son will make us mere
    Spectators at our own feast. But
    Who are we to complain? Dada knows
    He cannot wrestle, will he then preach restraint
    To his eager brother?

SARUMI: Kabiyesi.

DANLOLA: Well, I will not bear the offering
    Past the entrance to the mosque
    Only a phony drapes himself in deeper indigo
    Than the son of the deceased.

SARUMI [*with gratitude.*]: Kabiyesi!

DANLOLA: Dende!

[*He sweeps out, the others hurrying after him.*]

Immediately the Big parade drum is heard with its One–Two, One–
Two–Three, penny whistles blow to the tune of the Carpenter's Song
and the Carpenters' Brigade march in, uniformed, heavy mallets
swinging from their waists. They clear the stage and reset it for the harvest
scene—decorated dais, buntings, flags, etc. On a huge cyclorama
which completely dominates the stage, pictures are projected of various
buildings, factories, dams, etc., all clearly titled Kongi Terminus,
Kongi University, Kongi Dam, Kongi Refineries, Kongi Airport,
etc. Finally, of course, a monster photo of the great man himself.
They sing their anthem as they work, and form and execute a couple of
parade movements to the last verse or two.

We are the nation's carpenters
We build for Isma land
From the forests of Kuramba
They bring the timber wild
And we saw and plane and tame the wood
To bring the grains to light
Converting raw material
To 'Made in Ismaland'

Men of peace and honour
Are the Carpenters' Brigade
But primed for fight or action
To defend our motherland
We spread the creed of Kongism
To every son and daughter
And heads too slow to learn it
Will feel our mallets' weight.

Though rough and ready workers
Our hearts are solid gold
To beat last year's production
Is our target every year
We're total teetotallers
Except on local brew
For it's guts of toughened leather
That survive on Isma gin.

Our hands are like sandpaper
Our fingernails are chipped
Our lungs are filled with sawdust
But our anthem still we sing
We sweat in honest labour
From sunrise unto dawn
For the dignity of labour
And the progress of our land.

For Kongi is our father
And Kongi is our man
Kongi is our mother
Kongi is our man
And Kongi is our Saviour
Redeemer, prince of power
For Isma and for Kongi
We're proud to live or die!

The carpenters end with a march down-stage with stiff mallet-wielding arms pistoning up in the Nazi salute. Dende, also in uniform, is seen among them trying gamely to keep in step. Enter the secretary declaiming as he enters.

SECRETARY: Kongi comes! And with his Carpenters
Spitting fire on his enemies.
Comrades, our not-so-comrade comrades
Have their bottoms ready greased
For singeing, and do not know it. . . .
Hey . . . that is one new face, a very
Mouse among wildcats. Come here.
You seem at once familiar and yet
Completely out of place.

CAPTAIN: A new recruit. Newly defected
From the reactionary camp. You there!
Fall out!

SECRETARY: We must beware of spies.

CAPTAIN: I've put him through the standard tests.
He's no fifth columnist.

SECRETARY: Your name?

DENDE: Dende.

SECRETARY: The name is even more familiar.
Who was your last employer?

CAPTAIN: The king himself. Our mortal enemy.

SECRETARY: What!

CAPTAIN: A triumph for the cause sir.
It should be good for seven weeks
Of propaganda.

SECRETARY: Hm. That, I'll admit, is one way
Of viewing the matter. But look here
A joke is a joke; is he combat worthy?

CAPTAIN: Not as a fighter sir. But, as we are
Somewhat short on the muscle side—
The celebrations started a little early

For some carpenters, and that vigil
Beneath Kongi's hill of meditation proved
A disaster, a most debilitating
Orgy. Even these must nibble colanuts
To keep awake. So I thought, maybe
We could use him for odd jobs
And errands. I admit he is
A sorry looking crow, but at least
He swells the ranks.

SECRETARY: Well, I shall be on hand to assume
Full command, if it proves necessary.
I warn you, this is Kongi's day.
I've organised towards it for the past
Twelve months. If anything goes wrong
He'll have my head, but first I'll scrape
Your heads clean with your chisels
Without using lather.

CAPTAIN: I will die for Kongi!

SECRETARY: Let us hope that will not
Prove necessary. I'd better take this runt
With me. If any need arises, he will rush
My orders back and forth. Now once again
Bear it in mind—this is my last
Organising job before retirement
And I wish to retire to my village
Not to a detention camp. Is that clear?

CAPTAIN: We will die for Kongi!

SECRETARY: After my retirement. Now listen
All of you. Far be it from me to sun
My emblems in the square, but merit. . . .

DENDE: Is like pregnancy, never seen
But makes its proclamation.

SECRETARY: Well, well, well, the wonder actually
Boasts a voice. Tell me, why did you

Desert the palace? Were you bored
With swapping saws with that disgusting
Lecher?

CAPTAIN: We went parading past the palace
Just to show the flag you know
Suddenly there he was doggedly
Marching behind the ranks.
I shooed him off but he swore
He was resolved to be a carpenter.

[*They all burst out laughing.*]

CAPTAIN: Silence! 'Tention! As you were!

DENDE: I like the uniform. I asked Kabiyesi
To make me a uniform but he refused.

[*Again they fall to laughing.*]

CAPTAIN: Silence! 'Tention! The representative
Of our commander-in-chief, the Organising
Secretary, the Right Hand of Kongi
Our beloved Leader, will now address
The Carpenters' Brigade.

SECRETARY: Comrades, as I began to say, far be it
For me to sun my emblems but I am not
Without experience in the planning
Of moves and strategies on occasions
Such as this. And while it is true
That certain rules of strategy exist
In the manual of the Carpenters' Brigade
Yet is it the mark of genius when
A Field Marshall makes his own. The simplest
Part, you'll be surprised, is
The strategic disposition of your men
As laid down in your book of fundamentals
A man is either born to such basic
Know-how, or he should change his trade.
Even this warrior's progeny here

Can juggle men—what say you sir?
DENDE: Politicians, Kabiyesi used to say,
    Are as the seeds in a game of *ayo*
    When it comes to juggling.
SECRETARY: The boy approaches genius.
DENDE: Wise partymen must learn the cunning
    To crab and feint, to regroup and then
    Disband like hornets.
SECRETARY: I should have come to the same
    Training school as you. Now tell me,
    What are the realities of conflict
    As propounded by your royal sage?
DENDE: First, always outnumber the enemy.
SECRETARY: The man is a profound realist.
DENDE: And when outnumbered, run!
CAPTAIN: A fifth columnist, I knew it!
    He's here to demoralize the carpenters.
SECRETARY: Nonsense. Athletics is a noble
    Exercise. No need to be ashamed
    Or coy about it.
CAPTAIN: This is disgraceful.
SECRETARY: Nothing of the sort. You are privileged
    To learn today the ultimate realities
    Of war. As your Strategist and Field Marshal
    For this occasion, it shall be my duty
    To instruct you when events demand
    Its application. Come, you lion of Isma.
    [*They cross to the other side. He speaks to a group
    off-stage.*]
    It's safe to enter now. The stalwarts
    Have taken up position.
    [*Enter the Aweri. They take their places on the dais.
    Secretary goes off.*]
THIRD: Your speech is too short.

FOURTH: What are you talking about? It runs to four hours
and a half.

THIRD: Then you didn't listen to the news. The President
over the border has just spoken for seven. And you know
he fancies himself something of a rival to Kongi.

FOURTH: Disaster!

THIRD: Kongi won't like it at all. Can't you scribble something?

FOURTH: Impossible.

THIRD: He won't like it at all.

FOURTH: All right, all right. Don't keep on about it.

THIRD: But what are you going to do?

FOURTH: I'm dry. My brain is shrunk from hunger. I can't think.

THIRD: Add a diatribe on the condemned men.

FOURTH: It's down already. And I've run out of names to call
them.

THIRD: Include an exposition on Kongi's reasons for withdrawing the reprieve.

FOURTH: It's all down in the President's prerogatives.

THIRD: Then you've really had it.

FOURTH: Unless . . . you say you listened to the news . . .
anything about the one who escaped?

THIRD: He is still at large.

FOURTH: Then there is nothing I can add.

THIRD: I'm afraid not. [*With quiet malice.*] I'm afraid you've
really had it.

[*Re-enter Secretary with Dende.*]

SECRETARY: Something is not quite right.
My Number Seven sense refuses
To be silenced. Look here batman
Runner, aide-de-camp or whatever
You call yourself, go and find me
A vantage point for observation.
And remember friend, I have to keep
The entire square under observation

So, select some point quite distant
And reasonably protected. I hope
Your legs are in good training,
My instructions may likely be
Fast and furious. Well, get going man
And remember, not too near. My hearing
And eyesight are in top condition
And anyway, there are enough loudspeakers
To deafen the dead ... damn! another one
Of these brigades and organisations
Where on earth do I fit them?
[*Approaching, a male group singing to the rhythm
of cutlasses scraping on hoes.*]
Which reminds me, where are the
Women's Auxiliary Corps? The job
Of cooking the New Yam is theirs.
Lateness means trouble. Captain! Captain!
Where is your women's wing? Have I
Gone blind or are there really no signs
Of cooking preparations?

CAPTAIN: They should have been here to cheer in
My men. We intend to lodge a vigorous
Complaint.

SECRETARY: To hell with that part of it.
I've warned you, if anything goes wrong. ...

CAPTAIN: I had no time to check on them.
I was busy reviving what remained
Of the carpenters.

SECRETARY [*his fingers desperately stuck in his ears.*]:
And who are those metallic lunatics?

DENDE: It sounds like men from Prince Daodu's
Farming settlement.

CAPTAIN: Show-offs, that's all they are
Bloody show-offs.

SECRETARY: That noise, just because they won
    The New Yam competition. God, and that
    Is one more black mark against
    My performance today. I did my best
    To rig the results in favour of
    The state co-operatives, but that man
    Anticipated every move. And then his yam!
    Like a giant wrestler with legs
    And forearms missing. If only I had
    Thought of it in time, I would have
    Disqualified him on the grounds
    Of it being a most abnormal specimen.

CAPTAIN: Perhaps our women's wing have stayed away
    In protest.

SECRETARY: Make one more suggestion like that
    And I'll dress you and your carpenters
    In women's clothes, and make you do
    The cooking.

CAPTAIN: No, no, please . . . they are sure to come.
    I could send someone to hurry them
    If you. . . .

SECRETARY: Don't get nervous. I'd have a harder time
    Explaining why your carpenters
    Were not on hand. You stick to your job.
    Remember, your job is to guard the yam
    Every bit of the way. We don't want
    Some fatal spice slipped into it do we?

CAPTAIN: We will die for Kongi.

SECRETARY: Good. You have just volunteered
    To act as taster. I shall come personally
    And supervise the tasting—after the Yam
    Is cooked, and after it is pounded.
    [*The captain's jaw drops.*]
    Cheer up. Nothing is likely

To be tried. But it is just the idea
Of revenge which might occur
To our good friends the old Aweri.
So, keep good watch. You, run and stop
Daodu's yokels at the gate. I cannot
Let them in here—security reasons.
Only state approved institutions
May enter Kongi Square. Mind you
They may appoint a delegate, someone
To bring in the winning yam—only one!
[*Dende runs off.*]
I hope Daodu comes himself, at least
He can act civilized.
[*Royal drums and bugles. Enter Danlola, Sarumi, the old
Aweri and retinue. Secretary rushes to group them.*]
Kabiyesi! I had begun to rack my brain
For some excuse I hadn't used before
To explain your absence.

DANLOLA: I have only come to see our son's dance.

SECRETARY: Dance? Daodu? Does that one dance?
I know he shuffles about in that club
Of Segi's, but don't tell me he will
Actually perform in honour of Kongi.

DANLOLA: I do not know in whose honour
Daodu intends to dance or make others dance
But he bade us to the feast saying
Come see a new Harvest jig, so,
Here we are.

SARUMI: Our sons tell us we've grown too old
To dance to Kongi's tunes. We've come
To see them do better.

SECRETARY: I know his farm won the competition,
But as for dancing. . . . I mean, his men
Are not even permitted here. So how . . .?

DANLOLA: The bridegroom does not strain his neck
To see a bride bound anyway for his
Bedchamber. So let you and I wait
Like the patient bridegroom.

SECRETARY: Well, well, wonders will never end.
Winning that prize has really turned
Your prince's head ... oh, I trust. ... I mean
About the other matter, our agreement
Still stands? You will present the yam?

DANLOLA: If the young sapling bends, the old twig
If it resists the wind, can only break.

SECRETARY: You are not angry that the amnesty
Has been revoked? My ancestors will
Bear witness—I did my best.

DANLOLA: It's a foolish elder who becomes
A creditor, since he must wait until
The other world, or outlive his debtors.

SECRETARY: Live long Kabiyesi, we only await
Our women, and then the ceremony
Can begin at last.

[*Enter the women, singing, led by Segi who carries Daodu's cloak. They dance onto the stage bearing mortar and pestle, cooking utensils, a cloth-beating unit etc. They throw up their arms in derision and mock appeal to the world in general singing—*

Won ma tun gb'omiran de o   Oh here is a new wonder of wonders
Kongi ni o je'yan oba.   Kongi they say, will eat the king's yam

They curtsey to the seated obas, perform a brief insulting gesture as they dance past the Reformed Aweri. The Secretary has stood speechless at the sight of Segi, now recovers himself sufficiently to approach her. Segi signals to the women to stop.]

SECRETARY: What do you want here? You should not even
Dream of coming here.

SEGI: But I belong to the Women's Corps.

SECRETARY [*frantic.*]: Since when? I do not remember you
    Being remotely rehabilitated.

SEGI [*waving at the women.*]: Are all these approved people?

SECRETARY: Yes. They are all in the Women's Corps.

SEGI: They appointed me their leader. By a normal
    Democratic process.

SECRETARY: Captain! Get your men to veto
    The appointment.

SEGI: They also voted to ally with Daodu's Farm Settlement.
    We have deserted the Carpenters.

SECRETARY: Aha. There you have over-reached
    Yourself. You cannot do that unless
    By express dispensation of Kongi.

SEGI: Yes, but nothing can be done about that until after
    the Harvest, is there? We can seek approval—later—if it
    is still necessary.

SECRETARY [*goes near, near-pleading.*]: Woman what are you
    planning to do?

SEGI: Nothing. We heard Daodu and his men would dance for
    Kongi and we came to second his steps.

SECRETARY: Will you all stop saying that!
    What of a sudden is all this concern
    With Daodu's jitterbug. For one thing
    It is not on the official programme.

SEGI: His new yam won . . .

SECRETARY: The competition—yes! yes! We all know it.
    But so what? Is that enough excuse
    To turn my pageant into a Farmers' Cabaret?

SEGI: Have the farmers come?

SECRETARY: Yes, but I stopped them at the gate
    Which is exactly where they will
    Be left until the very end.

SEGI: I know. At the gate is where we promised
    We would welcome them.

[*to the women.*] Let's go.
Daodu may come in of course? He won . . .

SECRETARY: Yes he won, he won! Segi, I beg of you
Don't ruin twelve months of preparation. . . .
[*The women resume their song, dance out, leaving behind a
handful of them to attend to cooking preparations. Two women
begin a steady rhythm with the cloth-beaters, giving Daodu's
cloak a final sheen for the big occasion.*]
What can I do? He is entitled
To make a speech, and if like the Obas
He chooses to dance for Kongi
What is wrong in that? I only hope
It doesn't get out of hand, what with Segi's
Wild women abetting him.

CAPTAIN: Let him make a fool of himself.

SECRETARY [*slumping down wearily.*]:
Oh I don't know, I don't know at all.
Daodu is a cultured man. I had half-hoped
For some illiterate farm clod who would
Mumble the usual slogans and take
His farm stench off as fast as I chose
To cry 'Shoo'. But these new educated
Rascals! He's bound to show off and annoy
Somebody, or else make some ideological
Blunder, and then I get the blame.
[*Re-enter the women singing the same song and bearing Daodu
aloft. Others carry the farming implements which they have
taken from Daodu's men and use it to supply a noisy rhythm.
Daodu carries the winning yam above the triumphal entry.
They set him down, Segi takes the cloak from the women and
fits it around his shoulders.*]

SEGI: It is my turn to ask—you are not afraid?

DAODU: No. After all, only a little speech. Nothing need come
of it.

SEGI: It seems suddenly futile, putting one's head into the lion's jaws.

DAODU: Nothing may come of it.

SEGI: Nothing may come of it and then you will do something else, and that will be more final.

DAODU: Then pray that something does come of it.

SEGI: It is wrong to feel so selfish, but now that my father has escaped, I wish this plan was never made.

DAODU: I did not work for this merely for your father, Segi. At least, so I tell myself.

SEGI: I know. Forgive me.

DAODU: All I fear is that I won't be allowed to finish what I have to say.

SEGI: You will have enough time. They all have husbands, sons and brothers rotting in forgotten places. When they form a tight ring about you, only death will break it.

SECRETARY [*coming forward*]:
I might have known it. I never saw
A man make christmas over such a trifle
As the prize for a monster yam.

DAODU: It is a monster yam, it grew from Kongi's soil.

SECRETARY: Make your speech snappy, that's all
I ask of you. Five minutes at the most
Just be happy and honoured and all that
Stuff, and remember to feel proud to be
A son of Isma. If you exceed five minutes
It will be my duty to cut you off.
Captain stand by, here comes our Leader!

SECRETARY: Now! Ismite....

BRIGADE: Is Might!

SECRETARY: Ismite....

BRIGADE: Is Might!

SECRETARY: Ismite....

BRIGADE: Is Might....

SECRETARY: Now—One—Two—Three.

*An orchestra strikes up the national anthem. They all rise. Enter
Kongi, he stands under the flag until the end of the tune and is then
fussily led to his seat by the Secretary. Kongi selects his pose and
remains fixed in it throughout.*

*The Secretary signals frantically to Daodu to begin his presentation
speech and to make it snappy. Daodu fastidiously adjusts his robe,
takes out a small piece of paper.*

SECRETARY: Well, it looks like a short speech anyway, so that's
            not the danger. [*looks round nervously, sweating profusely.*]
            So where is it? Something is bound to go wrong. Some-
            thing always goes wrong.
            [*The women form a ring around Daodu with their pestles.
            Secretary stares in disbelief, especially at their hard, determined
            faces.*]
            I don't think I'll bother to find out. Dende, take me to that
            observation post. Something tells me this is the moment
            to start supervising from a distance.
            [*Half-runs off, dragging Dende along.*]
DAODU [*looking straight at Kongi.*]:
            An impotent man will swear he feels the pangs of labour;
            when the maniac finally looks over the wall, he finds that
            there, agony is the raw commodity which he has spent
            lives to invent.
            [*Stretches out his arms suddenly, full length.*]
            Where I have chosen to return in joy, only fools still
            insist that my fate must be to suffer.
            [*The tightness with which he has spoken thus far breaks into
            laughter; his arms come down.*]
            This trip, I have elected to sample the joys of life, not its
            sorrows, to feast on the pounded yam, not on the rind of
            yam, to drink the wine myself, not leave it to my ministers
            for frugal sacraments, to love the women, not merely

wash their feet at the well. In pursuit of which, let this
yam, upon which I spent a fortune in fertilizers and in
experiments with a multitude of strains, let it be taken out,
peeled, cooked, and pounded, let bitter-leaf soup simmer in
the women's pots and smoked fish release the goodness of
the seas; that the Reformed Aweri Fraternity may belch
soundly instead of merely salivating, that we may hereby
repudiate all Prophets of Agony, unless it be recognized
that pain may be endured only in the pursuit of ending
pain and fighting terror.
[*Handing over the yam to Danlola.*]

DAODU: So let him, the Jesus of Isma, let him, who has assumed
the mantle of a Messiah, accept from my farming
settlement this gift of soil and remember that a human life
once buried cannot, like this yam, sprout anew. Let him take
from the palm only its wine and not crucify lives upon it.
[*Kongi has remained rapt in his pose.*]

DANLOLA: I don't think he heard a thing.

DAODU: Don't let that worry you. In a few more moments he
will be woken up. And then it will be too late.

DANLOLA [*Looks up sharply, apprehensive, turns slowly round to
look at Kongi, shrugs.*]
As you wish.
[*Followed by the old Aweri, Danlola bears the new yam to
Kongi. Kongi places his hands over it in benediction and in that
moment there is a burst of gun-fire which paralyses everyone.
Kongi looks wildly round for some means of protection.
The Secretary rushes in a moment later, obviously shaken.
Hesitates, looking at Segi especially but drawn dutifully to
Kongi. He goes up to him and whispers in his ear. Kongi relaxes
gradually, swells with triumph. He begins to chuckle, from a
low key his laughter mounts, louder and more maniacal. His eye
fixed on Segi as a confident spider at a fly, he breaks off
suddenly, snaps an urgent instruction to the Secretary. The man*

hesitates but Kongi insists, never taking his eye off Segi. The Secretary slowly approaches her.]

SECRETARY: I wish you'd kept out of sight. Why did you have to let Kongi see you?

SEGI: I wanted him to. Anyway what is it?

SECRETARY: I would have waited but he says I'm to tell you at once. Your father . . . oh Segi what were you people planning for God's sake. What was he doing here?

SEGI: Go on. Have they caught him?

SECRETARY: Didn't you hear the shots?

DAODU: Oh God!

SEGI: He's dead?

SECRETARY [*nods.*]: What was he trying? Why was he here? Doesn't anyone know it's never any use.

SEGI: Go away.

SECRETARY: But why did he have to come back? Why didn't he just keep running, why?

DAODU: He's watching. He's watching.

SEGI: Let him watch. He shan't see me break.

DAODU: You mean to continue?

SEGI: Yes, let it all end tonight. I am tired of being the mouse in his cat-and-mouse game.

SECRETARY: I'm done for, I know it. I'm heading for the border while there is time. Oh there is going to be such a clamp-down after this. . . .

SEGI: Where have they taken him?

SECRETARY: In a schoolroom just across the square.

SEGI: I'll be back directly Daodu. Let everything go on as planned.

DAODU: Such as what? After what has happened, what?

SEGI: So he came back? Why didn't you tell me?

DAODU: I could do nothing to stop him. When he heard that the reprieve had been withdrawn . . . there was simply nothing I could do. He said he had to do it and no one else.

SEGI: It doesn't matter.

DAODU: We've failed again Segi.

SEGI: No, not altogether.

DAODU: What else can one do now?

SEGI: The season is Harvest, so let there be plenty of everything. The best and the richest. Let us see only what earth has fattened, not what has withered within it.

DAODU: What are you talking about? What do I do now?

SEGI: Sing, damn him, sing! Let none of our people know what has happened. Is it not time for Kongi's speech?

SECRETARY: Yes, he'll begin any moment. He's very much awake now.

DAODU: There should have been no speech. We failed again.

SEGI: Then forget he is there. Let the yam be pounded. I shall return soon with a season's gift for the Leader.

[*The women relieve Oba Danlola of the yam, take it away as Kongi rises slowly, triumphant.*]

KONGI: The Spirit of Harvest has smitten the enemies of Kongi. The justice of earth has prevailed over traitors and conspirators. There is divine blessing on the second Five-Year Development Plan. The spirit of resurgence is cleansed in the blood of the nation's enemies, my enemies, the enemies of our collective spirit, the Spirit of Planting, the Spirit of Harvest, The Spirit of Inevitable History and Victory, all of which I am. Kongi is every Ismite, and Ismite. . . . [*shoots out a clenched fist.*]

BRIGADE: Is Might. . . .

[*they beat on their drums and clash cymbals deafeningly.*]

KONGI: Ismite. . . .

BRIGADE: Is Might. . . .

SEGI: Now.

[*It is the signal for the feast to begin. A real feast, a genuine Harvest orgy of food and drink that permits no spectators, only celebrants. The dancing, the singing are only part of it, the centre is the heart and stomach of a good feast.*]

Ijo mo ko w'aiye o	At my first coming
Ipasan ni.	Scourges all the way
Ijo mo ko w'aiye o	At my first coming
Ipasan ni	Whips to my skin
Igi lehin were o	Cudgels on the madman's back
Kunmo lehin were o	
Aiye akowa	At my first coming
Ade egun ni o	A crown of thorns
Aiye akowa	At my first coming
Ade egun ni o	A crown of thorns
Iso lo g'aka m'ogi	The foolhardy hedgehog
Iso lo g'aka m'ogi	Was spreadeagled on nails

Mo ti d'ade egun	I have borne the thorned crown
Pere gungun maja gungun pere	Shed tears as the sea
Mo ti d'ade egun	I was spat upon
Pere gungun maja gungun pere	A leper's spittle
Omije osa	A burden of logs
Pere gungun maja gungun pere	Climbed the hunchback hill
Won tu'to pami	There was no dearth of yam
Pere gungun maja gungun pere	But the head of the firstborn
Kelebe adete	Was pounded for yam
Pere gungun maja gungun pere	There was no dearth of wood
Mo gbe'gi k'ari	Yet the thigh of the firstborn
Pere gungun maja gungun pere	Lost its bone for fuel
Mo g'oke abuke	
Pere gungun maja gungun pere	
Isu o won n'ile o	
Isu o won n'ile l	
Won gb'ori akobi le le	
Won fi gun'yan	
Igi o won n'ile e	
Igi o won n'ile e	

Egun itan akobi o
Ni won fi da 'na

Adeyin wa o	Now this second coming
Igba ikore ni	Is time for harvest
Aiye erinkeji	This second coming
Iyan ni mo wa je	Is for pounding of yams
Aiye ti mo tun wa	The mortar spills over
Iyan ni mo waje	Goodness abundant
Iyan yi kari	My body is balm
Ire a kari	I have come wife-seeking
Iyan yi kari	I am borne on laughter
Ayo a b'ori	I have come palm wine thirsting
Etu l'ara mi	My rheum is from sweet peppers
Ire akari	Contentment is earth's
Aiya ni mo wa fe	Ease for her portion
Ayo a b'ori	Peace is triumphant.
Aiye erin ni mo wa	
Ayo a b'ori	
Emu ni mo wa mu	
Ire a kari	
Ata ni mo wa ya	
Ayo a bori	
Aiye eso eso	
Eso ni baba	
Eso ni baba	

[*The rhythm of pounding emerges triumphant, the dance grows frenzied. Above it all on the dais, Kongi, getting progressively inspired harangues his audience in words drowned in the bacchanal. He exhorts, declaims, reviles, cajoles, damns, curses, vilifies, excommunicates, execrates until he is a demonic mass of sweat and foam at the lips.*
Segi returns, disappears into the area of pestles. A copper salver is raised suddenly high; it passes from hands to hands above the

*women's heads; they dance with it on their heads; it is thrown
from one to the other until at last it reaches Kongi's table
and Segi throws open the lid.
In it, the head of an old man.
In the ensuing scramble, no one is left but Kongi and the head,
Kongi's mouth wide open in speechless terror.
A sudden blackout on both.]*

HANGOVER

Again Kongi Square. It is near dawn. The square is littered with the debris and the panic of last night's feast. Enter Secretary, a bundle over his shoulder, dragging his tired body by the feet. Sitting seemingly lost beside the road, Dende; the Secretary does not immediately recognize him.

SECRETARY: Good friend, how far is it
    To the border? What! Well, well,
    If it isn't my bold lion of Isma.
    And what, may I ask, happened to
    The Carpenters' Brigade? Did they
    Receive my last instructions?
    Not that there was anything of a genuine
    Battle, if you get my meaning; nonetheless
    It was time to apply
    The ultimate reality of war—
    For their own sakes mind you—
    I hope you made that very plain
    To them. I know the ropes.
    To be there at all at that disgraceful
    Exhibition is to be guilty of treasonable
    Conspiracy etcetera, etcetera.
DENDE: There was no one to take my message
    They had all anticipated
    Your instructions.
SECRETARY: They lack discipline. A good soldier
    Awaits starter's orders. And you?
    What's happened to your Boy Scout movement
    I thought I ordered you to remove
    Your carcass far from the scene of crime.

DENDE: I don't know where to go.

SECRETARY: If you don't find somewhere soon
      There are those who might assist you.
      And their hospitality believe me,
      Is not to be recommended. I say,
      Is your problem by any chance
      Shortage of funds?

DENDE: Oh no, I spend nothing on myself and
      I carry all my savings with me
      Everywhere—as a precaution.
      As Kabiyesi himself would say....

SECRETARY: Oh? A quiet millionaire are you?
      Turn out your pockets.

DENDE: My pockets? What for?

SECRETARY: Don't blow your lungs boy. When a man
      Cannot even call briefly home to say
      Good-bye to his native land, then hope
      Remains his last luxury. Turn out
      Your pockets. As your late commander
      It is my duty to play censor
      To your battle-kit. Come on, come on,
      Let's see what keepsakes and
      Protection charms you wear to war....
      Aha, what's this? You haven't been
      Despoiling fallen warriors have you now?

DENDE: Those are rejected bits and pieces
      From the things we made for the king
      To take to harvest.

SECRETARY: I see ... a kick-back artist eh?
      And starting out so young. Hm,
      You carry quite a few trinkets around
      With you. Saving up for a bride-price
      I bet. Well, well, myself I am partial
      To silver, but I'll keep the copper bangle

Till your situation improves. Really,
You astonish me. A runner travels
Light, you are lucky you arrived
Unlooted from the battle front,
It seems there is one lesson of war
Your rogue king failed to teach you—Never
Carry your own ransom on your person—
Never!
[*Enter Danlola, furtively. He is also bundled with
his emergency possessions.*]

DANLOLA: Ah my son-in-politics, is the Big Ear
Of his Immortality still flapping high
In Kongi's breath?
[*Secretary quickly releases Dende, recovers from
his astonishment at seeing Danlola.*]

SECRETARY: Kabiyesi, don't mock a ruined man.

DANLOLA: If you are headed in that direction,
Then that way leads to the border.

SECRETARY: Do you suggest I am running away?

DANLOLA: Not I. Just the same, I'll be glad
To keep you company. If any man exists
Who wisely has prepared for such a day
It would be you. . . . Oh ho, is that not my Dende?

SECRETARY: Hold nothing against him. Few half-wits
Can resist a uniform.

DANLOLA: I hope he proved useful.

SECRETARY: The man is a philosopher. We have
Exchanged many areas of wisdom. Right now
He is my travelling companion.

DANLOLA: I don't see that you have anything
To fear. After all, no one could
Predict that surprise gift. The show
Was well organised, I mean, until that
Sudden business, all went well.

SECRETARY: I hope I shall live long enough
    To make good use of your testimonial.
    Went well! That is quite a mouthful!
DANLOLA: But it did go well. Well, as a hurricane
    Blows well. As a bush-fire on dry
    Corn stalks burns well, and with a fine
    Crackle of northern wind behind it.
    As a mat dances well when the man
    Is full of peppers and, with the last
    Guest departed, leaps upon
    The trembling bride. As I ran well
    When I took a final look at Kongi
    And began a rapid dialogue with my legs.
SECRETARY: And me. I never thought I had so much
    Motion between my legs.
DANLOLA: The others? What did the others do?
SECRETARY: I was by then too far away. Kabiyesi,
    It was no time to take notes for posterity
DANLOLA: What happens now? The hornets' nest
    Is truly stirred. What happens to
    The sleeping world?
SECRETARY [*sinking down.*]: Oh I wish I was the mindless smile
    On the face of a contented sow. Of a fat
    Contented sow. Fat I am, and uncharitable
    Tongues have labelled me a sow. But
    Contented? That is one uneasy crown
    Which still eludes my willing head.
    [*leaps up suddenly.*]
    What are we doing still sitting here?
DANLOLA: For now this is the safest spot to wait
    And Sarumi should join me soon—
    I hope. He's gone with some twelve toughs
    All volunteers—from among
    Daodu's own farmers. If he's not already

    In Kongi's hands, they'll abduct him
    Forcibly and parcel him across the border.
    And that woman of his.

SECRETARY: He is mad. And that woman, they're both
    Roadside lunatics. Even away from here—
    Take my advice, have them restrained.

DANLOLA: The strange thing is, I think
    Myself I drank from the stream of madness
    For a little while.

SECRETARY [*looks up anxiously.*]:
    It's getting light.

DANLOLA: I'll go and hurry them. You will . . . wait?
    Don't leave us behind I beg of you.
    When Providence guides my feet to a man
    Of your resourcefulness, I know
    Our safety is assured.

SECRETARY: Not Providence, Kabiyesi, but provisions.
    I only paused to glean a few emergency
    Rations from our young philosopher.
    But you are wrong—this idea you have
    Of travelling together, most imprudent.
    An entourage like that would be suicidally
    Conspicuous. Split, then meet once across
    The border—that would be my strategy.

DANLOLA: Of course, of course. You see, never would I
    Have thought of that.

SECRETARY: You'll learn Kabiyesi, you'll learn.
    Survival turns the least adaptable of us
    To night chameleons.

DANLOLA: Very true son. Well, I shall delay you
    No further. I hope Sarumi has been delayed
    By no worse than Daodu's stubbornness.

SECRETARY: Good luck sir. I shall precede you
    On active service, non-stop until

I am safe beyond the frontier. Oh,
What of this failed carpenter? Shall I
Take him with me—that is, if you don't mind?
DANLOLA: Oh, let him be. He's bound to do much
As the wind directs him, and anyway,
He is in no danger. He may even join
Our Royal Household Cavalry—in exile—
If we can find him a uniform.
SECRETARY [*undecided.*]:
Oh, well . . . I was only thinking . . . I mean
I could use a . . . yes, he could sort of
Earn his keep carrying this load for me. . . .
No, he'd only be a nuisance. I'm off.
Better hurry yourself, obstreperous old lecher,
I would wish you a speedy restoration
And a long and happy reign, but it would sound
Like mockery. See you at the border.
[*As he leaves, Danlola shakes his head in sad amusement.*]
DANLOLA: Safe journey. If I know you
The frontier fence will lose its barbs
At one touch of your purse;
There is already less corruption
In the air, even though your rear
Is turned.
[*He starts briskly back in the opposite direction. A mixture of the royal music and the anthem rises loudly, plays for a short while, comes to an abrupt halt as the iron grating descends and hits the ground with a loud, final clang.*]

BLACKOUT